It's not about the test

Compliance versus Commitment

It's Not About the Test:

Understanding data and creating assessment that actually works

Lisa Riegel, Ph.D.
Michael White
Bonnie Grimm
Lindsey Young

It's not about the test

© Copyright, Educational Partnerships Institute, LLC, 2015

Cover and illustrations by Brian Riegel

All rights reserved. No part of this book may be reproduced, stored in a retrieval system, or transmitted by any means, electronic, mechanical, photocopying, recording or otherwise without written permission from the authors.

It's Not About the Test:

Understanding data and creating assessment that actually works

Lisa Riegel, Ph.D.
Michael White
Bonnie Grimm
Lindsey Young

Contents

Introduction

Step 1 Data Driven or Data Dizzy?

Step 2 Map the Gap

Step 3 Testing to Improve Instruction

Step 4 What's Your Plan?

Step 5 Teach - Teach - Teach

Step 6 Testing to Prove Learning

Step 7 What's Your Backup Plan?

Compliance versus Commitment

References

Resources

Resources

Initial Data Reflection Sheet

Yearly Planning Guide

Monthly Planning Guide

Pretest Planning Guide

Pretest Analysis

Lesson Plan Template

Posttest Analysis

Pre- to Posttest Analysis

Implementation Checklists

Introduction

The accountability movement in education is not the latest fad that will run its course and end. Educators spend billions of public dollars a year, and being held accountable to show that we spent the money wisely and saw a positive impact is a fair expectation. I have never met a teacher who doesn't agree that we should have some way to show that we are effective. The trouble begins when we try to define HOW to measure our impact. Business models don't work, since students are not widgets. Isolating a teacher's singular impact is nearly impossible, because students are part of an integrated set of social and family systems that all impact their development. Learning is too complex to be reduced to a single number or color. The current methods of calculating teacher effects have been repeatedly proven to be produce unstable results. So what do we do?

Teachers need to answer the very fair question: "How do you know your educational institution is a good investment for public dollars?" This question, however, cannot be answered if we do not have the right data. We are currently in a system overloaded with big data points, but underequipped to use the data. We collect the wrong data, make poor attributions, and use the data as weapons. Part of the reason the accountability movement has been so bungled is due to some very serious and misinformed myths that are driving the legislative process. Teachers need to disprove these myths and answer the accountability question. This book is designed to help you do that.

Myth 1: Teachers can be evaluated to greatness

A mass exodus is underway. Education is losing teachers at an alarming rate, and we are not just losing teachers to retirement. About half our country's teachers leave teaching within five years (Ingersoll, 2014), and the rate of attrition is even higher in poor districts. In the most recent staffing survey, Ingersoll et al. (2014) learned that our teaching force is grayer, greener (meaning in their first five years of teaching), more diverse, female (in the next few years, 80% of our teachers will be women), and ready to leave. Why are so many teachers leaving? For the past two decades we have been pounded by tougher standards, budget reductions and public scrutiny. In the age of accountability, school leaders are now being asked to justify the impact of billions of tax dollars spent on public education. Unfortunately, we have not been able to adequately explain the impact of this funding. We have designed grading systems that measure compliance rather than mastery and set up teacher evaluation systems where everyone is rated as excellent. Despite numerous initiatives, our national and international assessment results remain flat and large achievement gaps persist.

Enter the politicians. In the absence of a solution, the legislators have created a broken system where more standardized test scores, value-added data and robust teacher evaluation systems are expected to explain quality. Mandates are unfunded, confusing, based on misattribution, and punitive. The teacher, the most important factor in educational growth and achievement, has become the boogeyman. This bad teacher boogeyman myth is appealing (Bessie, 2010). It prevents us from examining the myriad of contextual issues that affect student success, such as poverty, drugs, mental health issues, etc. It is much easier to simplify the issue to heroes and villains; geniuses and dopes; martyrs and slackers... good teachers and bad teachers.

New evaluation systems across the country and as a result of the national Race to the Top initiative have attempted to improve education by weeding out the boogeymen. Through quantifiable measures, we are attempting to evaluate teachers to excellence or to termination. For politicians who want to sound "tough on education," this system is very valuable. We can explain teacher quality through more specific observation protocols with descriptive rubrics and test results broken into three colors: red, green and yellow. Then we can assign neat labels, such as accomplished or proficient or developing to describe various types of teachers. The problem with this system is our results are consistently unstable. An excellent teacher one year can find him/herself at the bottom of the pack the following year. Teacher quality cannot possibly be that volatile. We just haven't found the right variables worth measuring to produce more stable teacher quality results.

We value what we measure and we measure what we value. Currently, that means we value what yields quantitative assessment data from big tests. While this data can be useful, it is not the most important data. Ninety-nine percent of assessment data is generated through teacher-created assessments and day to day work in the classroom. This book will help teachers learn a framework they can use to analyze the big data and apply findings in their classrooms. It will also help teachers learn to create reliable data through their own assessments and assignments. If we can learn to better design and interpret classroom assessment, and we can propose better variables for measuring how we know those billions of dollars have been put to good use, we can direct the future of policy. Otherwise, we will be victims of a system set up to generate useful sound bites for politicians.

Myth 2: A good teacher is a good teacher anywhere

What variables do we measure? What makes a successful school? This question is complex and interconnected, and it requires the unit of analysis to be the organization and not the individual teacher. Successful people are part of effective teams in sound systems. When Edison invented the light bulb, he had a team of 200 machinists, scientists, craftsmen and laborers. We often think of him as a solo inventor. In reality, Edison successfully led a huge team by dividing it into three to five member work groups. He expected each group to come up with one small invention every ten days and a big invention every six months. Edison's greatest invention may have been his system for creating inventions (Padgett, 2012).

It's not about the test

While recognizing individual excellence is important, it is a huge mistake to believe, or allow others to believe, that "a teacher can make or break a school." This attitude has led to the myth that school improvement can happen once you hire a few good people and get rid of the bad ones. Yet, if you look at large scale studies in everything from the automobile business to the airline industry, the evidence is clear: The "rule of good systems" trumps the "rule of good people." People's performance depends on the resources they have to work with, including the help they get from colleagues, administrators and the infrastructure that supports their work. It is practically impossible for even the most talented people to do competent, let alone brilliant, work in a flawed system. A bad system can make a genius look like a dope and a martyr like a slacker. In contrast, a well-designed system filled with average people can consistently achieve stunning performance levels (Pfeffer & Sutton, 2006).

Where would you rather work?

Consider how a teacher might do in each of the two systems described in a Harvard Educational Review article by Professor Susan Moore Johnson (2012). "Some schools were well-organized, purposeful, and supportive places for teaching and learning," says Johnson. "Teachers in such schools described how they had been hired in a thorough and informative process that allowed for a rich exchange of information between the candidates and their prospective colleagues and administrators. As candidates, they not only interviewed with the principal but also observed classes, talked with prospective colleagues, and sometimes were asked to teach sample lessons. These schools also ensured that new teachers' assignments matched their subject knowledge and preparation. They were not expected to teach in two subjects, mixed-grade classes, or to split their time between school buildings. Induction included regular opportunities to observe and work with experienced colleagues. They also were granted periodic release from administrative assignment, such as cafeteria duty, to observe their colleagues teaching. They received regular feedback about their instruction not only from their mentors and supervisors but also from the coordinators of their induction program."

Compare that to other teachers entering dysfunctional, under-resourced schools where they were hired at the last minute, isolated from colleagues, given challenging schedules and students, expected to teach out of their field, were rarely observed, and had few opportunities to observe other teachers.

Now imagine ranking these teachers using a common rubric and growth statistics without any consideration of the organizational health as a contributing factor. Then, publicize teacher rankings in the media and surround it with rhetoric about good and bad teachers. Why would anyone want to teach in challenging schools?

It's not about the test
Myth 3: A single teacher can be the hero and turn around failing schools

We all like the hero story. Many of us have seen movies like *Dangerous Minds* or *Take the Lead*, where teachers inspire urban youth. Or, we cried during *Dead Poets Society* when Robin Williams sparks his students' love of literature. Then there are classic biographical movies, such as *Stand and Deliver*, the story of Jaime Escalante or *The Ron Clark Story*. These hero myths make us believe that teachers can singlehandedly change education. They also make us believe that we must not have these superstar teachers if this kind of turnaround is not occurring. And while these heroics and martyrdom are admirable and can serve to energize teachers, their effects are not sustainable. If we set our sights on superheroes, we can lose the opportunity to leverage hard work among the average, real-life people. Average workers getting above average results is the mark of an effective and sustainable system.

When school leaders do not actively develop their staff and instead rely on a superstar to carry the load, they play a risky bet. Last summer I called a local principal whose staff and students had achieved amazing science scores on the state test. I was hoping to get his secret formula for success. Unfortunately, our conversation went like this:
Me: "Gary, so how did you get those great science scores?"
Gary: "It wasn't me; it was Kathy Harms, our science teacher, who did it. If she doesn't get pregnant or her husband doesn't get transferred, we'll probably do it again this year."

Well, I saw their science scores this year. Kathy, congratulations on your baby, or your husband's new job. Hope you are all doing well. That's right. Kathy did leave and science scores plummeted. How many of us know schools that are one or two pregnancies, transfers or retirements away from sliding from academic excellence to academic emergency? In contrast, a good system ensures that no one is indispensable and everyone is useful.

How many teachers are we going to ask to work sixty hours a week? And how many can we expect to score a 130 IQ on the Wechsler Intelligence Test? How many teachers are we willing to give up on, demote, or release before we take a good hard look at our school systems? Research consistently shows us that teacher effects on learning are not stable. This means that one teacher can have a great year followed by a poor one. Our system, however, is set up in diametric opposition to this reality. We judge teachers who have had a poor year to be poor teachers and we label teachers who had a good year as our superheroes. We're telling too many teachers they are not valuable anymore, that we're looking for someone younger or someone smarter. That's just wrong. Let's stop treating teachers as a bug in the system. We need to provide the teachers we already have with a better system. That's how we're going to turn our schools around.

It's not about the test

This book will provide a framework and process teachers can use to collaborate in meaningful ways so the data we generate, from both big tests and classroom assessment, can actually be used to improve student learning. This book will help build a system where average teachers can collaborate, work hard and achieve above average results.

The approach you will learn in this book is not radical. It is a simple, manageable and sustainable approach that has yielded great results for schools across the country. Hilliard is the 9th largest school district in the state of Ohio, serving nearly 16,000 students. Nearly a quarter of these students receive free and reduced lunch. Recently, the Ohio Department of Education released the official Local Report Card data for the 2011-12 school year. Of 832 schools and school districts ranked, Hilliard City Schools was ranked number one. Hilliard City Schools has earned the state's highest rating of "Excellent with Distinction" for the last five years.

Hilliard is just one place where teachers and school leaders have built a new system instead of looking for boogeymen. There are a lot more, including Madison County School District, Evergreen Park School District, Shelby City Schools and the Dioceses of San Diego, Joliet, Sacramento, San Jose, Charleston, Stockton and Phoenix.

After extensive analyses of factors that impact student achievement, John Hattie concluded that the single best way to improve schools was to organize teachers into collaborative teams, pre-assess to clarify what each student must learn and then analyze posttest results together so that teachers could learn which instructional strategies were working and which were not. In other words, balance big and small tests and treat teaching as a team sport (Hattie, 2009).

Based on the groundbreaking work of Hattie, as well as our own experience with successful schools, we have identified a seven step system which generates a culture of balanced assessment and data driven collaboration. Our system can help you use your collaboration time effectively and efficiently, so your system can support rather than suppress learning.

About the Authors

Lisa Riegel, PhD is the Executive Director of Educational Partnerships Institute, LLC, an educational consulting company that focuses on leadership development, teacher and principal induction, professional development and coaching, and community engagement.

Dr. Riegel consults with schools on setting up instruction and leadership systems that are efficient, measurable, and aligned with district goals. She also manages a Classroom Support resource for a national Transition to Teaching grant and builds online learning resources for novice teachers and principals in districts across the country. Ohio's FIP Your School project, for which she wrote facilitation guides to complement online modules on formative instructional practice, has won awards and recognition.

Dr. Riegel has extensive educational experience and has taught at the secondary, post-secondary and graduate level. She currently teaches courses for principal licensure and teacher leader endorsement at The Ohio State University. Drawing on her experience in the P-12 setting, Dr. Riegel translates theory to practice and helps educators understand the interconnectivity among initiatives.

Michael White is the Director of Educational Consulting Services, an educational organization in Cincinnati, Ohio. He is also a licensed pediatric psychologist.

Dr. White consults with school systems throughout the country on issues relating to standards-based instruction and assessment. A strong advocate of "assessment as instruction," he is the author of five books and numerous articles on standards, assessment, and effective schools. His web-based teacher resource, Learning Connection Online, was the National Staff Development Council's "Technology of the Year" award winner for 2003.

His books and presentations are the result of his work with small rural school districts, suburban school districts, and urban school districts throughout the country and are grounded in thirty years of teaching and coaching experience.

Bonnie Grimm is a national consultant. Bonnie's varied experiences in education include preschool curriculum and instruction, middle school and high school regular education and special education at the elementary level in both private and public school settings. Bonnie began her career as Director of Curriculum and Instruction for a private early childhood facility. Bonnie's experiences as both a regular education and special education teacher have provided her with an understanding of the challenges facing educators today and the importance of collaboration with specialists around data and best practices.

Bonnie is certified as a regular education teacher grades 7 to 12 and intervention

It's not about the test

specialist grades K-12. Bonnie was recognized in 2007 as a Martha Holding Jennings Scholar and is a regular presenter at conferences across the United States.

Lindsey Young is an elementary school instructional coach in the Princeton City School District. Prior to becoming an instructional coach, Lindsey taught grades 1 through 6 as a gifted intervention specialist, advanced math teacher, and self-contained general education teacher. Lindsey has been recognized as a leader in education and has received numerous awards, including winning the C3 Outstanding Cincinnati Teacher Award in 2006 and being a state finalist for the Presidential Award for Excellence in Mathematics and Science Teaching (PAEMST) in 2008. Lindsey has presented at National Council of Teachers of Mathematics and Ohio Council of Teachers of Mathematics regional conferences as well as facilitating professional development in Princeton and the Cincinnati area on topics such as mathematics instruction and assessment.

It's not about the test

Every August, eighth grade teacher Ira Flect makes the trip from his building over to the high school auditorium where the district's "Welcome Back Teachers Celebration" is held. Ira takes a seat in the back so he can beat the crowd back to the parking lot. It's his first day back from summer break so he still has loads of work to do to get his room ready for the school year. He slides down into his seat and thinks, "Twelve years, and it's always the same thing: The superintendent slide shows us how our kids scored on last year's state test and then prods everyone to do better. How about putting up a slide or two showing us how? Does he think that we've been holding back and saving our better lesson plans until he caught us?"

Data Driven vs. Data Dizzy

For the past 60 years educators have believed that the path to school improvement is paved with big tests, big slide shows and big test binders. This approach is not working. Achievement gaps persist and student achievement remains relatively flat. Isn't it time to have a serious conversation about why we continue to focus on big data as the golden ticket to school improvement? Big data can be useful when we are looking backward to prove that learning occurred, but the information is typically too much, too late and too vague to inform our day-to-day instruction. Teachers end up data-dizzy rather than data-driven. They'll say: What am I supposed to do? How should I change to make sure my students succeed? This test data doesn't give me anything specific to help me decide what and how to teach this group of students? I know they have trouble with fractions but what specific skills are they missing? That is what I need to know. And all the work we do with our big tests, like SMART Goals, Action Plans, and Data Walls seem to be more for public relations than practical application.

We are not saying big tests should be expelled from schools. There are loads of ways they can be useful. Big tests, sometimes called Summative Assessments, are given periodically to check if learning has occurred. They help us answer the question at the end of the quarter or year: "Did the students master the skills taught?" Many teachers and parents associate big tests only with standardized tests like the Iowa Assessments or state achievement tests, but "big" tests are also used at the district and classroom level. Big tests at the district level might be called quarterly, short-cycle, or benchmark assessments. At the classroom level, they might be called final exams or end of course exams.

All of these tests have certain features in common:
- Big tests show, at a particular point in time, student learning relative to a collection of skills
- Big tests occur after instruction every few weeks, months, or once a year
- Big tests are usually viewed as something separate from teaching
- Big tests are often what teachers use to determine grades

It's not about the test

Big tests allow students' progress to be tracked over the years. For example, if a student scores in the 75th percentile in the sixth grade and the 86th percentile in the seventh grade on the Iowa Assessments, you can see that the child is gaining ground relative to grade-level peers. Big tests, like the Iowa Assessments or state achievement tests, are also used by administrators to evaluate the effectiveness of the curriculum and textbooks. They are beginning to be used to evaluate the effectiveness of teachers.

Big tests are useful, but they do not provide sufficient information to improve instruction and increase student learning. Teachers need strong assessment literacy to use big test data, know the limits of what these data can do for you, and to create classroom assessment to fill in the gaps.

How to Use Your Big Tests

Big tests are a great tool for providing teachers with a mission. Many schools have big missions that state goals about building lifelong learners or maximizing student potential. These missions help schools determine what they value about their role in educating children. They are very important, because they can inform system decisions, including community partnerships, parent engagement, and human resources. Missions derived from big test data are more specific and are directly related to learning content. They are not bumper sticker slogans, but specific statements that explain your goals, and they can provide a sense of clear purpose and even adventure. A good mission can re-shape assumptions, guide practice, and inform collaboration.

Here's a mission you might have heard about. On November 21, 1963, President Kennedy spoke in San Antonio and introduced our mission to the world. The United States would build the Saturn rocket and be the first country to put a man on the moon. Days before, his advisors had warned President Kennedy not to announce this mission. After all, they cautioned, if the space program effort failed it would be politically embarrassing, perhaps even political suicide. The President took into account the counsel of his advisors, but not in the form that might be expected.

Before announcing the Saturn mission to his audience, President Kennedy described how young boys in Ireland would make their way across the countryside, and when they came to an orchard wall that seemed too high and too hard to climb, they took off their caps and tossed them over the wall - and then they had no choice but to follow their caps. Kennedy went on to say, "This nation has tossed its cap over the wall, now we have no choice but to follow it. Whatever the difficulties, they will be overcome. We will climb this wall. We will climb this wall with safety and with speed - and we shall then explore the wonders on the other side." A mission is a formal and public statement of what you are going to do. Once you have said it, you have thrown your cap over the wall and will have to go after it.

It's not about the test

District and school level missions are more general and multifaceted. Teachers classroom missions should be very targeted and directly related to using all available information to improve teaching and learning. Big tests can help teachers find and hone their classroom mission, so it is directly related to what students need. Using big data from state or national assessments to find your mission is like drilling down through a series of folders on your computer's desktop to find a specific file. Clicking on a general folder takes you to a more specific folder; another click takes you to your specific file. "Drilling Down" through your big test data uncovers the specific skills you need to more effectively teach your students. Drilling down from an overall test area to a domain of related skills and then to specific skills provides clarity as to what students struggle with and are not able to do. Drilling down identifies the "what" for teachers: What skills do your students need to develop? What lessons are not hitting their mark? How do I redesign my approach to ensure students learn that content? This is your mission. Teachers who have a mission will always be more successful than teachers whose understanding of what they need to do is murky or directed from a central office initiative.

Drill Down to Determine Your Success Stories and Your Honest Bad News

We can enhance or destroy students' desire to succeed in school swiftly and permanently when we misuse and overemphasize big tests. This is why it is imperative teachers find the success stories and share them with their students. Your big test results contain plenty of success stories. Find them! These results help students see what worked, so they can repeat those habits and behaviors. Drill down through the overall results and find the two domains on which the students performed best. Then examine those skills. Let's say your math test results indicate your sixth grade class scored highest on the Geometry domain and the Statistics domain. Make a big deal out of these relative strengths. Take the time to ask yourself, your colleagues and your students. "Why are we so strong on these standards?" Spend time talking and thinking about what you did well. And whatever you and your students did to achieve these scores, do it again!

Next, it's time to look at your honest bad news. Ineffective schools will often try to hide, distort or make excuses for their bad news. They will assign blame factors outside their control, such as parents, poverty, or transient students. Don't spend time and energy trying to determine who got you into this mess or who is to blame. Instead, drill down and determine your one or two lowest domains.

Look at those specific skills. See box below. Instead of setting goals for author's craft, you can determine which skills in that domain were not learned to mastery and focus on those as your mission.

Drilling Down Through the Iowa Achievement Tests

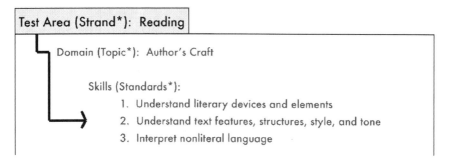

Once you establish your mission, tell everyone you know. The more people to whom you announce your mission to get higher literary devices and elements and interpretation of nonliteral language scores, for instance, the more people you will have asking you how it's going, prodding you along and giving you useful advice. The most effective schools are places where teachers are noisy and nosy and travel in packs.

Some people will object to the idea of prioritizing skills to double down on one or two domains. They'll stamp their feet, send letters to the editor, and say we should focus on all the domains and 45 skills. We are not suggesting you abandon all lessons except the ones that address your bad news areas. Instead, we are saying the bad news domains should become your focus for the year. Revise lessons, spend a bit more time, relate the weak areas to other areas in which students perform well. If we are going to think deeply and explore new teaching ideas thoughtfully, then the logical and unavoidable solution is to focus on a few skills each semester, trimester or quarter, skills taken from the lowest domains. It's better to select and accomplish two or three goals than to attempt twenty, thirty or forty goals and achieve none.

Most of the strategies you develop and the changes you make as you work with your honest bad news skills will transfer and impact your teaching of other skills, as well. And, taking time to celebrate your good news first will ensure you don't stop using effective lessons or approaches.

See It in Action (Uncovering Your Success Stories and Honest Bad News)

English Language Arts
To see how you can use the data from Iowa Assessments to drill down from the domains to the skills, let's demonstrate using Amanda's report below. Her class item report from the Iowa Assessment can help her find her good news and honest bad news for her fourth grade students.

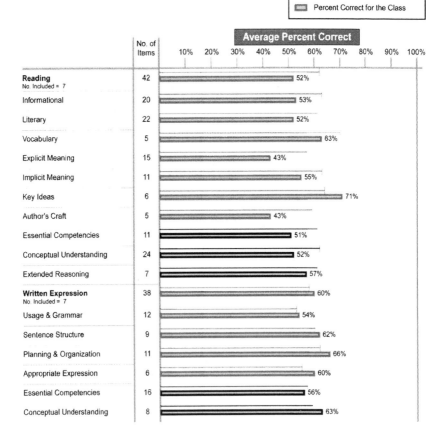

It's not about the test

Her success stories are quickly apparent by looking at the percentages correct for each section of the tests. Key Ideas was the clear winner with 71% correct, a higher percentage than the national norm. By drilling down to the subtests she is able to see that ability to identify central ideas and their supports are success stories. She makes a note so that she will remember to use these strengths when tackling the weaker skills.

Her "honest bad news" skills are also evident from a quick examination of the percentage scores. Two areas stand out as needing work, Author's Craft and Explicit Meaning, with only 43% correct in both areas. Amanda next uses her Class Item Response Record (See Class Item Response Record below) to drill down and identify the following skills within Author's Craft; understanding literary devices and elements, understanding text features, structures, style or tone, and interpreting non-literal language. This becomes Amanda's set of skills to tackle, her mission. Since explicit meaning is also an area of weakness, she decides to include opportunities to practice with understanding and recognizing stated information, along with Author's Craft. She will spend additional instructional time on these skills and revise her lessons.

Amanda records her success stories and honest bad news on her data reflection sheet to help with planning. Your grade level team might consider creating a format like Amanda's that works with your PLC or Teacher Based Team formats. Reflection sheets should have concrete details. Note that Amanda put the percen

Initial Data Reflection Sheet

Name: Amanda Dillon	Subject: Reading/Grade 4	Date 8/2015
Success Stories		
71% correct on Key Ideas • Identify central ideas and their support • Connect or extend ideas		
Honest Bad News		
43% correct Author's Craft • Understand literary devices and elements • Understand text features, structures, style, or tone • Interpret nonliteral language 43% correct explicit meaning • Understand and recognize stated information		
My mission: To draw on the strengths my students show in their ability to pull out key details and to focus more time on helping them understand the way author's use literary devices, text features, style, tone, and nonliteral language to communicate the key details. I will also ensure students can understand and recognize explicit information.		
Next steps 1. Consider why key ideas were a strength and how I can use these strengths to help improve the bad news 2. Create new materials to focus on Author's Craft and embed the skills into multiple lessons		

Mathematics

State Achievement Assessment Results: 8th Grade Math

Ira Flect, an eighth grade teacher, can use the same process to drill down and create a mission based on mathematics assessment data. He is excited about the results in several areas, especially Statistics and Probability, where 84% of his students are proficient.

Domain	Score Bands % Below	Score Bands % Proficient	Score Bands % Above
Number System	37	59	4
Expressions and Equations	12	79	9
Functions	10	74	16
Geometry	6	74	20
Statistics & Probability	9	84	7

Three other domains, Expressions, Functions, and Geometry are also success stories, with more than 70% of his students' proficient. He just changed to include more direct instruction with modeling and performance tasks, and he believes these changes are paying off. His students are on track in four out of five domains.

Ira notices Number System is still an area of weakness, with only 59% of his students proficient. Ira knows he will need to change his approach this year, so he drills down through Number Sense to better understand the skills his students are missing. Teaching these skills will become his mission.

Initial Data Reflection Sheet

Name: Ira Flect	Subject: Math – Grade 8	Date 8/2015
Success Stories		
84% proficient in Statistics & Probability Expressions, Functions, & Geometry all above 85% proficient or above		
Honest Bad News		
59% proficient in Number System • Know that the numbers that are not rational are called irrational • Use rational approximations of irrational numbers to compare the size or irrational numbers, locate them approximately on a number line diagram, and estimate the value of expressions		
My mission: To draw on the strengths my students show in their abilities in Statistics, Probability, Expressions, Functions, and Geometry to help them understand rational numbers and how to compare them, locate them and estimate the value of expressions.		

Next steps
    1. Determine why students struggle with irrational numbers and consult with other teachers about how they teach the concepts.
    2. Create new methods to reinforce irrational numbers into other lessons designed to teach the other domains.		

It's not about the test

These reflection sheets can be useful for teams to use as they plan for the semester. Teachers can share their results and can discuss each other's practice. This targeted collaboration can help generate new and creative ways teachers can approach instruction. Further, when teachers share their missions with each other, they can help support each other by finding materials, sharing ideas, and troubleshooting issues. This kind of collaboration and discussion around data can also satisfy requirements for PLCs or Teacher Based Teams.

The next chapter, Map the Gap, will discuss how teachers can work together to achieve their missions.

Now you try:

What is summative data and what summative data do you collect in your building or district?

What is the purpose of "drilling down?"

Examine Amanda's data and her Initial Data Reflection Sheet. Do you agree with Amanda's findings? What other conclusions would you draw from her data?

Apply: Create your own Data Reflection Sheet using big data from assessments given in your district.

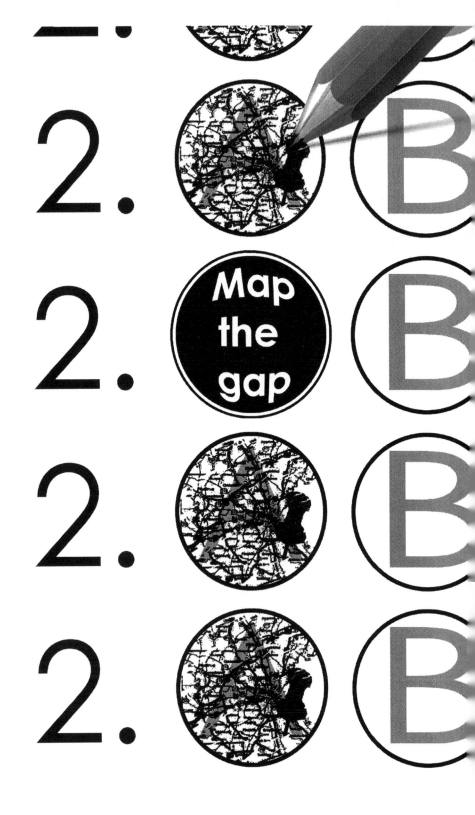

It's not about the test

Today, most schools have some sort of road map that describes what skills will be taught, when these skills will be taught, and how much time will be spent to get the desired results. You might call this map an academic calendar, a pacing guide, or, behind the principal's back, "that binder I haven't opened in two years."

Without a system, it's easy to discount the importance of these road maps. And that is exactly what many of us do. Often, by the middle of the year, teachers have abandoned their maps and set off in different directions. Consequently, central office administrators send out the frantic e-mail across the district stating that, "the curriculum maps are posted on the district's web site. Please use these maps or take them off the school's web site. Parents are asking why we're not following them!"

It's a shame maps are not more universally utilized because they are a great way to break a year into smaller, more manageable time chunks. Maps help you with the purposeful planning of instruction of skills instead of slip-shod coverage or, worst case, omissions because you just ran out of time. Maps visually display the planning and teaching time that is available to you for each standard. Without such a tool, teachers can sometimes spend too much time on units they enjoy teaching, and too little time on other topics. Or, they can insert fun activities, such as making Mother's Day gifts or holiday crafts that take too much time and prevent them from getting to parts of the curriculum. Having a mission based on data can help teachers stay focused and avoid this mistake, because they will be reflective about how they are teaching each skill. Having a map can also help make collaborative time more useful, because teachers will be focused on the same skills at the same general time. Much more creative approaches can be taken if teachers are in sync. For example, while reading a common book, such as To Kill A Mockingbird, teachers can create multiple options for students to engage with the text, and then each teacher can focus on one area and students can rotate through the classes. One teacher might focus on poetry related to a theme in the book. Another might focus on activities regarding structure and craft. Another might focus on research topics related to the book's content. These teachers can focus their lessons and take extra time to create something fantastic, because they do not have to prepare everything themselves. Students can be grouped in creative ways to allow for more choice and interaction among classes, and data can be examined collectively at the end to see which approaches had the biggest impact and what changes should be made in the future. At the elementary level, teachers can do much more ability grouping and targeted intervention with students, because they can examine pre-test data together and divide students by the specific skills they are teaching rather than divide them by general reading levels. Curriculum map can be a central tool to enable this type of collaboration and creativity.

The drawback of curriculum maps, however, is that they are often created by central office administration and completely unrelated to data. Teachers treat them as if they are etched in granite and cannot be adjusted to respond to student data. In our system, your honest bad news should drive the way you approach mapping your year. If your data tell you that your students are not getting the hang of irrational numbers, you need to have flexibility to lengthen the time you spend on those concepts. When maps are created by teachers based on data, really creative approaches to instruction can happen. If the teachers are all focused on similar concepts at the same time, they can be creative with ability grouping and differentiating instruction. They can also compare classroom assessment data and make adjustments in real time. Too often we wait until the big test data come back instead of making sure we are addressing student mastery and confusion in real time.

Meeting each student's educational needs requires constant vigilance and adjustment. Consider a barge trying to park in port. The captain starts turning and preparing to dock ten miles out and then makes numerous minor corrections based on the data, such as the wave currents, weather conditions, speed, etc. He is constantly monitoring a number of data points during the process. Teachers should be using the classroom assessment data in the same way. Just as we don't want to wait until the last minute to think about parking the barge and risk hitting the dock and sinking, we don't want to wait until the high stakes assessment to determine if our students are on track. Big test results should not be surprising to anyone, because teachers should be constantly checking and assessing student growth and understanding. We should be checking for gaps and mapping them with every unit.

See It in Action (Map the Gap)

English Language Arts

Amanda and Kay, the other fourth grade teacher, sit down to review and adjust the district's curriculum map to allow for intentional instructional planning around their honest bad news, the domain "Author's Craft." Amanda and Kay first examine their tests results. The Iowa Assessments identify the following skills as part of Author's Craft:
- understand literary devices and elements
- understand text features, structures, style or tone
- interpret nonliteral language

When Amanda and Kay look at the district map, they notice these skills are supposed to be taught as part of Unit 2 covering an eight week period using both literary and informational text (See Yearly Planning Guide: 4th Grade Reading).

It's not about the test

Yearly Planning Guide: <u>4th Grade Reading</u>

Week of...	Unit/Topic	Standards	Notes
8/20/12	Unit 1: Key Ideas & Details	RL 4.1, W 4.1, W 4.2	4 day week
8/27/12		RL 4.1, RL 4.2, W 4.1, W 4.2	
9/3/12		RL 4.2, W 4.2	4 day week
9/10/12		RL 4.3, W 4.2	
9/17/12		RI 4.1, W 4.1, W 4.2	
9/24/12		RI 4.1, W 4.1, W 4.2	
10/1/12		RI 4.2, RI 4.3, SL 4.3	
10/8/12		RI 4.3, SL 4.3	
10/15/12		Summative Assessment	Friday late start
10/22/12	Unit 2: Craft and Structure of Literature and Informational Text	RL 4.4, W 4.2	4 day week
10/29/12		RL 4.5, W 4.2	
11/5/12		RL 4.5, W 4.2	
11/12/12		RI 4.6, W 4.2, W 4.9b, SL 4.1a	11/16 preassessment on RI 4.5
11/19/12		RI 4.5, W 4.9b, SL 4.1a	
11/26/12		RI 4.5, W 4.9b, SL 4.1a	2 day week, Thanksgiving
12/3/12		RI 4.5, W 4.9b, SL 4.1a, e	
12/10/12		RI 4.5, RI 4.6, W 4.9b, SL 4.1a	
12/17/12		Summative Assessment	Friday late start
12/24/12		Winter Break	
12/31/12			
1/7/13	Unit 3: Integration of Knowledge & Ideas	RL 4.7, W 4.1, L 4.5	
1/14/13		RL 4.7, W 4.1, L 4.5	
1/21/13		RL 4.9, W 4.3	4 day week
1/28/13		RL 4.9, W 4.3	
2/4/13		RI 4.7, W 4.2	
2/11/13		RI 4.7, RI 4.8, W 4.2, L 4.3	4 day week
2/18/13		RI 4.8, W 4.2, L 4.3	4 day week
2/25/13		RI 4.9, W 4.2, L 4.3	
3/4/13		Summative Assessment	
3/11/13	Unit 4: Text Range and Differences	RL 4.10, W 4.4, 5, 7, 8	RL, RI, Sci, SS integrated research project
3/18/13		RL 4.10, W 4.4, 5, 7, 8	literature selection supports research
3/25/13		RL 4.10, W 4.4, 5, 7, 8	
4/1/13		RL 4.10, W 4.4, 5, 7, 8	4 day wk; choose research support
4/8/13		Spring Break	
4/15/13		W 4.8, SL 4.1d, SL 4.2	4 day wk; organize info; peer review
4/22/13		W 4.8, SL 4.1d, SL 4.2	State testing (Mon-rdg, Thurs-math)
4/29/13		W 4.8, SL 4.1d, SL 4.2	State testing (Wed-writing)
5/6/13		RI 4.10, L 4.2, SL 4.1d	
5/13/13		RI/RL 4.10, W 4.6, SL 4.1, SL 4.4	
5/20/13		Summative Assessment	present oral & visual presentations
5/27/13	Transition to 5th Activities		4 day week

It's not about the test

Because these lessons are not scheduled until November, Amanda and Kay decide to use their collaboration time to plan assessments and instruction. Additionally, they discuss how they can preview these concepts while they are teaching the units scheduled before the Second Unit. These previews can help prime students for the information, so they are ready to hit the ground running when Unit 2 begins. Finally, they adjust the curriculum map to allow for extra instructional time for the Author's Craft unit. They consider how interruptions, vacations or other programs might impact their instructional time (See Monthly Planning Guide: 4th Grade ELA – NOTE: this example uses the Common Core State Standards reference numbers).

Monthly Planning Guide: 4th Grade ELA Reading

Week of...	Standards and Summary of Plan
11/10/14	CCSS ELA Literacy RL 4.6, W 4.2, W 4.9b, SL4.1a • Completion of the unit RL4.6 • Unite closure with reading activity of 1st and 3rd person narratives. Identify and place examples on anchor chart • Concluding activity: Students use graphic organizer and complete to demonstrate differences between 1st and 3rd person narratives • Readings: "Mary's Summer Vacation" pg 78-83 and "A Day at the Beach," pg 110-114 • Pretest for RI 4.5 on 11/7
11/17/14	CCSS ELA Literacy RI 4.5, W 4.9b, SL 4.1a • Students will review text features and identify text features such as word banks, glossaries, use of heading and sub headings, charts, graphs, maps and keys (added due to results of pretest) • Students will read texts with chronology or cause and effect organizational structures. Students will identify structures and information in texts. • Concluding activity: Interactive reading of "The Water Cycle." Students will identify text features used to organize piece. Discus suse of cause and effect as an organizational structure. In independent work, give second article on water cycle that uses steps to organize information. Assign written response to prompt, "Which method did you find the most informative or helpful and why."
11/24/14 Only 2 days of school this week	CCSS ELA Literacy RI 4.5, W 4.9b, SL4.1a • Students will review examples of Chronology and Cause and Effect structures. Place examples on anchor chart • Students will read texts with problem-solution organizational structure. Use graphic organizers to identify structures and information in texts
12/1/14	CCSS ELA Literacy RI 4.5, W 4.9b, SL 4.a, c • Students will work with texts that use comparisons as an organizational structure and review methods of organizational structure in informational text. Place examples on anchor chart. • Concluding activity: Students will read one article comparing Shawnees and Miami Tribal Cultures and another article describing the challenges and solutions facing Native Americans in Ohio. Students will identify organizing structures and why the author chose that structure to share information.

Mathematics

Eighth grade teacher, Ira Flect's mission is to improve his students' performance with the Number System, his honest bad news from last year's test. Only 59% of his students were proficient in Number System. First, he needs to examine the yearly curriculum map to see where these skills are taught, when they are scheduled to be taught, and what will be taught before. He's going to develop some new activities to address his honest bad news, and he wants to talk to his colleagues to get their input. He is the only eighth grade math teacher in the building, so he has been meeting with math teachers from grades six and seven. This vertical teaming approach can be very valuable and help Ira understand how the sixth and seventh grade teachers are teaching the skills. This information can be very helpful for Ira as he develops a pre-test to see what skills students retained from the previous year. A well-designed pretest can yield very useful data. Sometimes just understanding the language and vocabulary previous teachers used can help make the pretest more valid, as fewer students will miss questions because they didn't understand the expectations. A pretest should also have stretch, and we will discuss that in the next chapter.

Ira checks the district's curriculum maps and notes on his calendar the full instructional weeks versus interrupted weeks (i.e., holidays, conferences, pep rallies). The district has allotted two weeks in October for instruction on fractions, but Ira believes he will need more instructional time to ensure students understand the Number System (See the Yearly Planning Guide: 8th Grade Mathematics).

It's not about the test

Yearly Planning Guide: 8th Grade Mathematics

Week of...	Unit/Topic	Standards	Notes
8/20/12	Intro. to Transformations	8.G.A.1	4 day week
8/27/12	Unit 1: Transformations	↓	
9/3/12	↓	↓	4 day week
9/10/12	Unit 2: Congruence	8.G.A.2, 8.G.A.3	
9/17/12	↓	↓	
9/24/12	Unit 3: Similarity	8.G.A.3, 8.G.A.4, 8.G.A.5	
10/1/12			
10/8/12			
10/15/12	↓	↓	Fri. late start; begin Unit 4 on Fri.
10/22/12	Unit 4: Rational/Irrational #s	8.NS.A.1, 8.NS.A.2, 8.EE.A.2	4 day week
10/29/12	↓	↓	
11/5/12	Unit 5: Pythagorean Theorem	8.G.B.6, 7, 8	
11/12/12	↓	↓	11/16 preassessment on RI 4.5
11/19/12	Unit 6: Functions	8.F.A.1, 2, 3 & B.5	
11/26/12	↓	↓	2 day week, Thanksgiving
12/3/12	↓	↓	
12/10/12	Unit 7: Intro. to Linearity	8.EE.B.5 & 6, 8.F.B.4 & 5	
12/17/12	↓	↓	Friday late start
12/24/12		Winter Break	
12/31/12			
1/7/13	Unit 8: Statistics and	8.SP.A.1, 2, 3, 4	
1/14/13	Probability	↓	
1/21/13	↓	↓	4 day week
1/28/13	↓	↓	
2/4/13	Unit 9: Nonlinear Functions	8.F.A.3, 8.F.B.5	
2/11/13	↓	↓	4 day week
2/18/13	Unit 10: Linear Equations	8.EE.C.7a-b	4 day week
2/25/13	↓	↓	
3/4/13	↓	↓	
3/11/13	Unit 11: Systems of	8.EE.C.8abc	RL, RI, Sci, SS integrated research project
3/18/13	Linear Equations		literature selection supports research
3/25/13	↓	↓	
4/1/13	Unit 12: Exponents and	8.EE.A.1, 3, 4	4 day wk; choose research support
4/8/13		Spring Break	
4/15/13	Scientific Notation		4 day wk; organize info; peer review
4/22/13	↓	↓	State testing (Mon-rdg, Thurs-math)
4/29/13	Unit 13: Geometric	8.G.A.5	State testing (Wed-writing)
5/6/13	Relationships	↓	
5/13/13	Unit 14: Volume of Cylinders,	8.G.C.9	
5/20/13	Cones, and Spheres	↓	present oral & visual presentations
5/27/13			4 day week

It's not about the test

Ira is afraid this won't be enough instructional time, especially for some of the new activities he wants to try. He adjusts the timing to reduce the days he spends on Congruence. His students scored very well on Congruence problems, so he is confident he can reduce instructional time there and add it to his unit on Irrational Numbers. By taking time to create a more detailed map for tracking his bad news, Ira was able to prepare ahead and better able to manage the extra time he was going to spend on his Bad News skills. He creates his monthly map for October to ensure that he has adequate assessment, preparation and instruction time. (See Monthly Planning Guide: 8th Grade Mathematics – NOTE: this example uses the Common Core State Standards reference numbers).

Monthly Planning Guide: 8th Grade Mathematics

Week of...	Standards and Summary of Plan
10/6/14	CCSS Math Content 8 G.A.3, 8.G.A.4, 8.G.A.5 CCSS Math. Practice MP3, MP4 • Vocabulary: dilations, translations, rotations, reflections, coordinates • Explore transformations of 2 dimensional figures by using coordinate planes • Lesson Idea: Human Coordinate Plane Activity
10/13/14	CCSS. Math. Content: 8 G.A.3, 8.G.A.4, 8.G.A.5 CCSS Math. Practice: MP3, MP4 • Vocabulary: similar, exterior angles, parallel, transversal, triangle • Continue developing transformations of 2-dimensional shapes by working with similar shapes. Have students prove why shape is similar
10/20/14	CCSS. Math. Content: 8 G.A.3, 8.G.A.4, 8.G.A.5 CCSS Math. Practice: MP3, MP4 • Extend the content from the previous two weeks to include facts about the angle sum and exterior angles of triangles, parallel lines and transversals, and the angle-angle criterion for similarity of triangles • Summative assessment at the end of the week
10/27/14	CCSS. Math. Content: 8 NS.A.1, 8.NS.A.2, 8.EE.A2 CCSS Math. Practice: MP6, MP7 • Vocabulary: irrational, rational • Understanding rational versus irrational numbers • Converting between fractions and decimals • Finding rational approximations of irrational numbers (e.g. on a number line)
11/3/14	CCSS. Math. Content: 8 NS.A.1, 8.NS.A.2, CCSS Math. Practice: MP6, MP7 • Continue work on rational and irrational numbers • Summative assessment at the end of the week

Now you try:

List the benefits a yearly plan has for you or your team.

What are your local challenges to creating and using a yearly plan?

How do you currently account for the interruptions, such as holiday breaks, professional development days or late starts, etc. and what adjustments do you make to your maps?

Examine how Ira and Amanda planned their monthly guides. Use your district curriculum map and create your own monthly plan that targets a specific skill you identified in your mission.

Generate a list of ways your team can be more creative if you are all in sync and using the monthly maps.

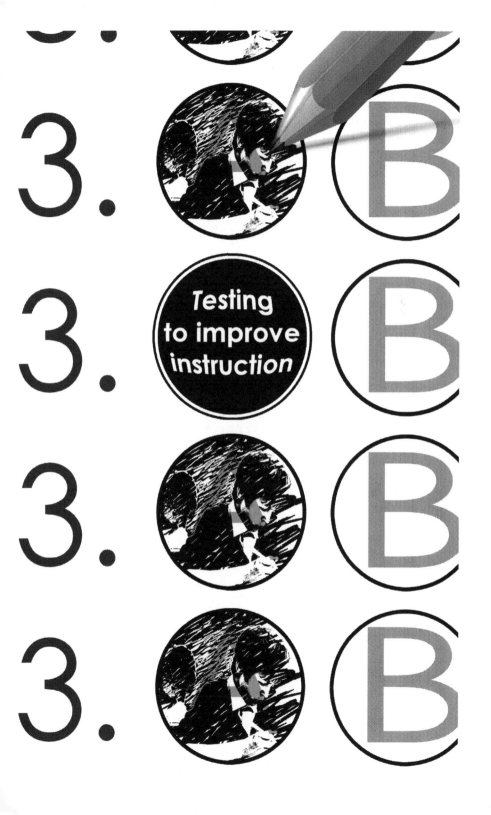

It's not about the test

"Pretests! I never heard of anything so foolish! Testing students before I even teach the lesson is a waste of time. We haven't even covered the material yet. Of course students aren't going to get the answers right. This is crazy, wasting my time and using up test questions on this," shouts Ken Tankerous.

But, 45 minutes later, in the teacher's lounge reviewing the results of that stupid pretest Ken was forced to give, he is muttering to himself, "What the heck is going on? One of my pretest questions simply asked which fraction is larger – 1/3 or 1/4. Most of these kids picked one fourth because 4 is bigger than 3. Are they trying to kill me? Some of these kids don't know the difference between fractions and whole numbers. And we're going to start adding and subtracting fractions next week! They will be lost, and I'll be wasting our time. Darn it, I'm going to have to change my lesson."

Altering his lesson, the one he had bronzed in 1987, is not a prospect Ken relishes, but he knows he cannot proceed with his plan if most of his students have not mastered the pre-requisite knowledge. Perhaps adding and subtracting fractions is one of Ken's Honest Bad News skills, and perhaps this pretest can help him figure out that the best lesson in the world isn't going to work if the students do not yet understand fractions. Ken is now realizing that classroom assessments – diagnostic, formative and summative – are all part of a balanced assessment system that is crucial to student success.

Balanced Assessment: Big Tests and Little Tests

Chapters 1 and 2 asked you to examine data from Big Tests, summative tests. These tests have a specific function, which is to measure the learning that should have occurred. They are the tests that can help us find our overall mission, as they can help us see where we have failed to lead students to mastery in specific skills. Pretests serve a different function. While big tests can tell us what students don't know, the pretest can tell us why they don't know it. They help us understand how much information students have retained and what holes we need to plug before we move on. A well designed pre-test can help teachers determine exactly where students are in the progression of learning a skill. Pre-tests provide a sense of direction for teachers, as they help them determine where to start and how to group students who are on track, need accelerated, or need remediated. Big tests prove learning while pretests improve learning (Stiggins, 2004).

A balanced assessment system has a pre-test to determine where to start, formative assessments to gauge progress, and summative assessments to measure growth and mastery. Sound and effective assessment design is a non-negotiable skills teachers need. However, many teacher preparation programs fail to help teachers learn to develop good assessments. In this chapter, we will help you think about how you develop a good pretest and in Chapter 6, we will discuss post test design and administration.

What Makes a Good Pretest?

Pretesting, as its name implies, is intended to measure students' skills and interests before instruction begins. It should provide you with precise information regarding:

1. What students know?
2. What students don't know?
3. What students want to know?

Pretests should not be painful to build, take or score. Good pretests have only handful of carefully designed items. Their purpose is to gather information about a student's readiness to learn the skills/standards that are scheduled to be taught. Pretests uncover student misconceptions and, more importantly, teacher misassumptions. Pretests are scored, but not graded. Their purpose is not to grade student performance. They indicate their level of readiness and guide your planning for the unit and your approach to grouping students and differentiating instruction. For example, a student who demonstrates mastery of the geometry skill you are about to teach can have the opportunity to "compact" out of the traditional learning sequence while the other students learn the grade level geometry skill. Students scoring lower on the pretest would be provided skill building activities to reach the necessary readiness level. Pretesting is about knowing your audience, your learners.

The key to developing a pretest is to know the vertical articulation of your content. For example, to learn how to add and subtract, students need to understand quantities. Which number is bigger? If they do not know that, the idea that adding yields a larger sum than the parts will not make sense. To create a pretest, teachers should have a few problems that ask students to identify which number is bigger. Perhaps they put numbers in order from smallest to largest or perhaps they compare two numbers. Then, the test should have a couple addition problems. Finally, you might put a double digit addition problem on the pre-test. The results of this test will tell you which students need more help with quantities, which students are ready to learn to add, and which students will need enrichment. This information is enormously valuable and makes teaching more efficient, because the teacher can immediately address what each student needs.

The pretest can be a great time to help figure out not only what a student knows, but also what a student wants to know. The word relevance pops up all over educational literature and in professional development. In addition to the questions that address the skills, you might survey students quickly to see if they have ideas on how the concept you are teaching is applied in real life or have them share times they have seen their parents use the skills. Their answers will help you gather important information about what they value. For example, one student might say they had to learn about ratios when they were scuba diving, because they needed to know the percentages of gases to prevent getting the bends. Once you have a better idea of what interests your students, you can create lessons or select reading material that relates to student's lives and arouse their curiosity. I guarantee that most students will not say they are very interested about what happens when two trains are traveling toward each other at 45 mph. Remember, while you are wondering if they are "getting it" your students are usually wondering why they are "doing it"! Often, they will "get it" and retain it better if they know "why" they are doing it.

One of the most important benefits of pretests is that they pave the way for true collaboration, as opposed to collaboration lite (event planning and committees). When teachers have useful data generated from well-designed pretests, teacher meetings have a sense of urgency and a data driven focus. Without the data, teachers can only speak in generalities and assumptions. The data allow true collaboration that can have an impact. Pretest data over time can also be incredibly informative for vertical teams. They can inform the teachers in the grade below about how well the students retain what they have learned. If there is low retention, teachers might consider how they are making the information relevant and "sticky." Pretest data can be an impetus for reform that has significant impact on teaching and learning.

In addition to informing improvement in teaching practice, pretests inform accountability measures. In this era of questioning the value and effectiveness of teachers, it is critical that teachers can show students are learning in your classroom. Most states now use the term value-added, borrowed from business, to indicate student progress and teacher effectiveness. In order to truly establish what value you have added to your students, a pretest must be given to determine the starting point for you and your students. Then, after the lesson, a posttest can be given to determine what your students actually learned. The difference between the two scores is the "value" that has been added by your teaching. If Ken never gave his pretest, he might be preparing and delivering gold star lessons, but his students may still fail, because the lessons were too far above their skill level. Pretests can help teacher make sure they know where students are at the beginning, so they can measure how much they have grown by the end of the unit.

Some teachers will complain about pretests because they expect students to score a zero. This kind of complaint is rooted in the faulty assumption that students know nothing and come to the class with no prior instruction. Standards are scaffolded and educational content is spiraled to such a degree that almost nothing your students are expected to learn each year is completely new. Even content-heavy subjects like science and history have repeated concepts. Consider how many times students are taught the scientific method or the various branches of government. Additionally, it is possible, in fact probable, that your students have learned skills independent from the school system If we want lifelong learners, shouldn't we expect and celebrate learning outside of class?

It's not about the test

Remember, nearly everyone gets the History Channel and many students are carrying smart phones that connect them to just about any information they need. So, it becomes important for you to determine what your students know before instruction. Second, a good pretest will not only contain one or two grade level questions, but also one or two questions below grade level. Remember, the goal of a pretest is to determine where your students are so that you can design the lesson they need.

See It in Action (Developing and Administering Pretests)

One of Amanda's and Kay's "bad news" skills is scheduled for instruction beginning November 17th and continuing for two and a half weeks. Both teachers want enough time to cover the skills included in "organizational structure" such as cause/effect, problem solution and text features. Since this is a persistent problem for their students, they need to know more about what their students know and don't know. They decide to give the pretest early so they will have time to review students' answers, discuss the results at their grade level meeting and make any changes to the lesson before beginning it on the 17th.

As part of their pretest they want to make sure the students have the prerequisite skills needed to begin instruction of newer skills. They look up the standard for this same skill for the grade below, 3rd grade. This is easy with the Common Core State Standards, since the numbers align nicely. For example, RI 3.5 (Reading Informational Text, Craft and Structure, Standard 5) is the prerequisite skill for RI 4.5 (Reading Informational Text, Craft and Structure Standard 5. (Unfortunately, this easy alignment with similar numbering is not used in math and may not be aligned in other standard systems.)

Pretests need to be short, so they decide to focus on how text is organized as the targeted skill. In planning the pretest they use one question based on the third grade standard and two based on the fourth grade standard. They also include one short answer question to tease out any guessing. Amanda designs the prerequisite third grade question, while Kay does the fourth grade questions. Teachers need strong content knowledge to prepare good pretests, because they need to understand how the skills progress from one grade to the next. They also need to match test items to the level of complexity in the standard, so they are able to gather good evidence of whether or not a student has mastered a concept.

It's not about the test
Here are some key considerations when planning a pretest:

1. Include items that assess the prerequisite skills needed.

2. Consider the best format for the question. Match the level of thinking required to the question task. For example, you do not need to write a short answer or extended response to determine if a student knows a vocabulary word. However, you might need a short or extended response to gauge a student's ability to identify a theme and justify their thinking.

3. Consider how many items are needed to determine a student's abilities. Do you need ten similar math problems or can three carefully constructed problems designed to identify faulty thinking give you the information you need?

4. Save a bank of questions teachers can share. If you find students seem to always miss a particular item, examine that item to see if it is a poor question or if this is a skill that the team is not teaching well.

5. Make each question specific to only one standard. Teachers can still compare results even if they have used different questions, so long as the questions are asking for the same level of thinking and are directly measuring a specific standard.

6. Look for tests that have been created by vendors. As long as you know the specific skills being assessed in the test, you can use these as pretests. See "From Eggs to Wings: A Science Project as a sample.

From Eggs to Wings: A Science Project

by Karen Sebesta

Here is a project that will let you see how a tiny white egg becomes a beautiful monarch butterfly. This project takes few supplies and very little work. It will take a few weeks to complete, but it is worth the wait. You will need an adult to help you.

You will need:

- 1 small container (jar or box)
- 1 large container (jar or small fish tank)
- 2 pieces of net or other see-through material
- 1 rubber band
- strong tape
- spray water bottle
- soil
- milkweed plants and leaves

Stage 1: Making Your Egg Container

You will collect monarch eggs in the small container. First, measure the opening of the small jar or box. Cut enough net material to cover the container. Place some **moist** soil in the bottom of the container.

Stage 2: Finding the Monarch Eggs

Ask an adult to take you to an open field where milkweed plants grow. Be sure to take the small container with soil, the piece of material you cut, and the rubber band with you. The monarch butterfly lays one egg per milkweed plant on the underside of the leaves. If there is more than one egg on a leaf or plant, then more than one butterfly has laid eggs there.

The monarch egg looks like a tiny white igloo with dark lines. When you find an egg, remove the entire milkweed leaf it is on without disturbing the egg. Collect one or more eggs. Place the leaves with eggs in your collection jar along with a few extra leaves. Place the small piece of material over the top of the jar and hold it in place with the rubber band.

FUN FACT
The reason you find monarch eggs only on milkweed leaves is that milkweed is the only food the caterpillar eats!

At home, move the soil and leaves from the small container to the larger one. Keep the soil moist with your spray water bottle. Use the larger piece of net material to cover the large container. Tape the net on, but leave about six inches without tape so that you can reach into the container.

Stage 3: Watching the Caterpillar Grow

In about six days, a tiny white worm will hatch from the egg. This is the caterpillar or **larva** stage. The worm will quickly eat the leaf that the egg was on. About six hours later, it will develop black, yellow, and white stripes.

Every few days put fresh milkweed leaves into the container for the caterpillar to eat. Over the next two weeks the caterpillar will grow and shed its bright skin four or five times, until it is about two inches long. Caterpillars make a lot of waste, so you will need to clean the container often and wash your hands well with soap after doing the cleaning.

It's not about the test

Stage 4: Your Caterpillar Changes Again!

When the caterpillar finishes growing, it will move to the top of the container. It will then spin a fine, silky mat and hang from it. It will hang in the shape of a J. The caterpillar will begin to change into a **pupa**. Its skin will turn greenish and **transparent**.

You will see the pupa change over the next few days. It will slowly become darker as the butterfly forms inside. Soon you can see the butterfly's bright colors through the pupa skin.

Stage 5: A Butterfly Appears!

After about two weeks the butterfly will shed the pupa skin. At first its wings are wet and are stuck to its body. The wings are bright orange or yellow. They are trimmed with black and have white spots. In a few hours the butterfly's wings will dry so that it can fly.

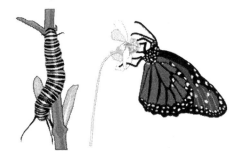

Monarch caterpillar   **Monarch butterfly**

Stage 6: Saying Goodbye

It is now time to let this beautiful butterfly fly away. Ask an adult to take you to the milkweed patch where you found the butterfly egg. Release the butterfly and watch it fly away to meet other monarchs that live there. The monarch is ready to start the butterfly life cycle again.

GLOSSARY

larva (LAR-vah) – the worm or caterpillar stage in an insect's life
moist (moyst) – slightly wet; damp
pupa (PYU-puh) – the quiet cocoon stage in an insect's life
transparent (trans-PARE-unt) – see-through

---

1. How does the author arrange the information in this passage?

    A. with step-by-step directions
    B. with a cause and its effects
    C. with a definition and examples
    D. with a comparison between two things

2. Which is the correct order of a butterfly's life cycle?

    A. egg, larva, pupa, butterfly
    B. larva, egg, pupa, butterfly
    C. egg, pupa, larva, butterfly
    D. larva, pupa, egg, butterfly

Directions: Please write your answer below the following question.

3. In this passage, where can you find the definition of the word **Larva**?

It's not about the test

Mathematics

After reviewing the seventh grade standards for rational and irrational numbers, Ira develops his pretest with good stretch, meaning he includes questions to assess prerequisite skills, some eighth grade skills and some above grade level skills. This mix of questions will allow him to determine the skill levels of all the students in his class. Below is his plan. Compare his plan to his pretest.

Pretest Planning Guide: 8th Grade Mathematics

Standards	Date of pretest	Prerequisite skills	Test questions Low	Test questions Moderate	Test questions Challenging
CCSS.Math.Content: 8.NS.A.1, 8 NS.A.2 CCSS.Math practice: MP6, MP7	10/6/14	Converting a rational number to a decimal (from 7.NS.A.2d)	6	3	1

It's not about the test

Rational and Irrational Numbers Pretest/Posttest   Name

Directions: Please choose the best answer choice for each of the following questions.

1. A goldfish was $4\frac{1}{4}$ inches long. Which of the following is another way to express $4\frac{1}{4}$?

   A. $\frac{4}{17}$
   B. $\frac{4}{9}$
   C. 4.14
   D. 4.25

2. What is the decimal equivalent of $\frac{7}{20}$?

   A. 0.03
   B. 0.035
   C. 0.3
   D. 0.35

3. A carpenter measures a shelf that is $32\frac{1}{8}$ inches long. Which of the following shows an equivalent measurement?

   A. 32.8 inches
   B. 32.18 inches
   C. 32.125 inches
   D. 32.018 inches

4. Kim needed to change many fractions into decimals. When she was finished, what did she MOST LIKELY find?

   A. All the decimals were repeating.
   B. All the decimals were terminating.
   C. None of the decimals terminated or repeated.
   D. Some of the decimals terminated and some repeated.

5. Diana writes the number 8 on the board. Which of the following numbers is closest in value to 8?

   A. $\sqrt{32}$
   B. $\sqrt{48}$
   C. $\sqrt{65}$
   D. $\sqrt{88}$

6. During a classroom activity, Mr. Franklin wrote this phrase on his overhead.

   the cost, c, in dollars for x people to see a movie at the Rivera Theatre

   After this phrase was read, Mr. Franklin asked his students to determine which set of numbers in the real number system would BEST describe the values for each variable in his phrase. Which student response is correct?

   A. The cost, c, will be a rational number, and the number of people, x, will be an integer.
   B. The cost, c, will be a rational number, and the number of people, x, will be a whole number.
   C. The cost, c, will be an irrational number, and the number of people, x, will be a natural number.
   D. The cost, c, will be a whole number, and the number of people, x, will be a rational number.

It's not about the test

Rational and Irrational Numbers Pretest/Posttest   Name _____

7. Which list gives examples of irrational numbers?

   A. $7, 11, 13$
   B. $-42, 0, 21$
   C. $\sqrt{2}, \sqrt{5}, \pi$
   D. $0.\overline{3}, 0.\overline{12}, -0.\overline{6}$

8. Rachel is trying to locate $\sqrt{15}$ on the number line.

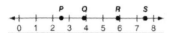

She said that point S best represents $\sqrt{15}$. Which statement is the best choice to explain *how* Rachel is correct or incorrect?

   A. Rachel is incorrect because 2.47^2 is about 15, and point S is greater than 2.47.
   B. Rachel is correct because 15 divided by 2 is 7.5, and that is the location of point S.
   C. Rachel is incorrect because 3^2 is 9 and 4^2 is 16, and point S is much greater than a point halfway between 3 and 4
   D. Rachel is correct because 7^2 is 14 and 8^2 is 16, so point S, which is halfway between 7 and 8, would represent $\sqrt{15}$.

9. The area of a circular rug is 16π square feet. This number is either rational or irrational. Which of these statements is correct?

   A. It is irrational because 16π is not a whole number.
   B. It is rational because 16π can be written as $\frac{16\pi}{1}$.
   C. It is rational because 16π is the same as 16×3.14.
   D. It is irrational because 16π cannot be written as the quotient of integers.

10. Which fraction can be written as the repeating decimal $0.\overline{859}$?

    A. $\frac{774}{900}$
    B. $\frac{900}{851}$
    C. $\frac{990}{859}$
    D. $\frac{859}{999}$

43

Now you try:

What is the purpose of a pretest and how is it different than a formative or summative assessment?

What valuable information can be gained from a pretest?

Look at the list of considerations when designing a pretest. Analyze one of your own pretests to see if you have addressed each.

Work with your colleagues to design a pretest for your next unit. Consider how you will use the results as a grade level team and in vertical teams.

It's not about the test

Front loading instruction with a good pretest is critical to being an efficient teacher and to avoiding the frustration of realizing that some of your students have no idea what you are talking about or the frustration of spending hours creating an amazing lesson only to discover the students already know the content. What a total waste of time and effort!

When teachers create effective pretests and use the results to design instruction, learning accelerates and students are more engaged. If you are teaching a ninth grade geography lesson on weather stations and discover that many of your students don't understand latitude and longitude, you can save a lot of wasted time if you adjust your lesson and bring them up to speed. Pretests give you the information you need to design relevant and effective lessons.

Pretest data can be used to sort students into groups: those students who need remediation; those who are ready for your lesson; and those who already know the content and need enriched content. You can also use the data to help you mine the misconceptions students have. This can help you determine where in the process they are getting lost. For example, students may be missing math problems because they still need help remembering the order of operations. You can also use pretest data to form student dyads or teams, where students have complementary strengths and weaknesses. Finally, you can shuffle and share students. Kay, for example, might do an enrichment activity with all the proficient and above students while Amanda works with the not yet proficient students on the skills they need to access the standard.

In the last chapter, you learned about creating pretests. The quality of your pretest will greatly impact what you can do with the data it generates. Assuming you have a great pretest, you can use the data to inform your lesson planning and delivery which will accelerate student growth and achievement.

See it in Action (Pretest Analysis)

English Language Arts

Analyzing their pretest results, Amanda and Kay are pleased that when the story is read aloud, 85% all students are able to answer question number 1 (the prerequisite 3.5 standard) correctly. 10% of their students were able to answer all the questions correctly.

Amanda discovers that 3 of her students are not reading on grade level, and are not able to answer any questions without having text read aloud to them. In both classes students are having a difficult time with organizational structure. Their pretest results tell Amanda and Kay what their students know, don't know and want to know. Now they are ready to design their lesson.

It's not about the test
Pretest Analysis: 4th Grade Reading

This process is used for each standard you were assessing in the pretest. Notice there is more than one teacher listed. This is a great process to go through as a grade level team. You can get an accurate snapshot of where all students are in the grade and make instructional decisions as a team.

Domain/Topic/Standard RI.4.5 and RI.4.6			Date: 11/10/14	
Class Name	No understanding	Major Misconceptions or Errors	Minor Misconception or Errors	All Correct – Needs Enrichment
Mrs. Dillon	2 students: EJ, WB	7 students: AL, JJ, GV, EF, DR, BD, PR	10 students	1 student LG
Mr. Sera	1 student: MC	11 students: JD, IR, FL, PA, DD, WE, FW, QO, MM, PP, DC	7 students	1 student: LY
Totals	3	18	17	2

Pretest strengths, misconceptions, and student interests

Strengths:
- When story was read aloud, 85% of all students were able to answer question 1, the pre-requisite 3.5 standard correctly
- 50% answered question 3 correctly and were able to recognize organizing structure when steps were included
- 40% were able to use a glossary to answer question
- 10% of the students were able to answer all questions correctly

Misconceptions or concerns with relevant instructional strategies (back up plan):
- 3 students are not reading on grade level and could not answer any questions without text read aloud (These students will be provided with instructional reading level materials to practice new skills before working with grade level texts)
- 15% (6 students) missed question 1. All 6 incorrectly chose definition as the organizational structure. This demonstrates a misunderstanding of subheadings and glossary and their use in this text. (Recommended additional small group work reviewing definitions of text features and use within text. Practice with selecting features, structures 1 week during unit)
- 5 students could not answer question number 2, were not able to use sub headings and bolded terms to identify order of butterfly development. (Additional small group practice using text features in order to answer questions/gain information from text, 1 week during unit)

Additional recommendations:
- Modify introduction in lesson plan to include both review of definitions and examples along with practice identifying examples of organizational structures
- Create schedule and possible staff to work on both re-teaching activities and extending activities.
- High yield strategy of similarities and differences will be used to reinforce concepts

Interests:
- Majority of students indicated they would like to read about Indians.

Mathematics

Ira's pretest results show that 15% of his students are not able to find simple fraction and decimal equivalents. His original lesson would not have started at this level. His pretest scores are all over the place. Some students missed the prerequisite skills question, most scored in the middle and 5% of his students got all the multiple choice questions correct. For these students he will have to provide enrichment that goes deeper into this topic. Since Ira is the only 8th grade math teacher, you will notice his analysis includes only his classes.

Pretest Analysis: 8th Grade Mathematics

This process is used for each standard you were assessing in the pretest.

Domain/Topic/Standard 8.NS.A.1, 8.NS.A.2			Date: 10/6/14	
Class Name	No understanding	Major Misconceptions or Errors	Minor Misconception or Errors	All Correct – Needs Enrichment
1A	1 students: Samantha	8 students: Ryan, Ali, Jake, Dion, Asia, Jon, Charlie, Cayon	9 students: Lily, Monica, Aaron, Trinity, London, Kara, Luke, AJ, Matt	1 student: Kelly
1B	2 students: Alex Zane	10 students: Vince, Marty, Karen, Rose, Hannah, Kamyra, Layla, Joe, Annie, Ed	8 students: Rosy, Sam, Sarah, Colin, Nick, Nathan, Connor, Miles	1 student: Liza
Totals	3	18	17	2
Pretest strengths, misconceptions, and student interests				

Strengths:
- 85% of students could select the correct decimal equivalent for 4 ¼ and 32 1/8 (questions 1 & 3)
- 80% of students can identify rational versus irrational numbers (questions 7 & 9)
- 5% of the students got all multiple choice questions correct. Enrichment that goes deeper into this topic will be provided. For the posttest, they will maintain their score and have a performance task

Misconceptions or concerns with relevant instructional strategies (back up plan):
- 15% of students are not able to find simple faction and decimal equivalents. Practice fluency with fraction-decimal equivalents using a calculator and folding in flash card intervention. Teach mini-lesson with those students on how to convert by dividing numerator by denominator. This will help students who incorrectly chose answers B & C.

It's not about the test

Now you try

What instructional changes would you make if you were Amanda or Ira?

How will you use your pretest data in the future?

Work with your colleagues to create a format you will use to analyze your pretest data in the future.

It's not about the test

Your pretest sets you up to create a perfectly matched lesson plan, but even after all your preparation, students might react to your new and improved lesson in different ways than you anticipated. The timing may be off, students may be confused, frustrated or bored with your delivery. Reflective teachers take notes on what works and what doesn't. They are in a constant state of reflection and revision. Writing down your reflections ensures you do not forget and make the same mistakes twice. It also reminds you of the aspects of the lesson that worked well, so you will retain them for years to come.

Teachers collect a variety of information, including:

- A list of questions you anticipated students would have

- A list of questions you did not anticipate, but will prepare to address in the future

- When students seemed to get bored or animated by the lesson

- Information you had to repeat several times

- What materials you used or what materials you would have liked to have

- How well students were able to describe what they learned through exit tickets or verbal feedback

- What information from the lesson seemed to be interesting to students, what aspects generated the most inquiries, or what parts led students to want to learn more

- Connections students made between their own lives and the content of the lesson

- Classroom management data during the lesson – how many students were off task or needed corrected

It's not about the test

See It in Action

English Language Arts

Read over Amanda and Kay's lesson plan.

Lesson Plan: 4th Grade Reading ELA

Learning Targets
I can identify the overall structure of an informational text. (RI 4.5). I can read and use informational text to gather information (explain how author uses evidence to support points in a text.) (W 4.9b). I can participate in a variety of collaborative discussions and follow rules of group work. (SL4.1a&b).

Introduction
- A review list of text features and definitions are listed on board. (i.e., word banks, glossaries, headings, sub-headings, maps, keys, charts).
- Students will examine examples of texts with text features placed on desks.
- In collaborative groups, students will begin to identify examples of text features.
- Review definitions and have students take turns sharing selections and examples. Place correct responses on Anchor Chart.

Direct Instruction/Mini Lesson
- Share with students that focus on new unit will be identifying how organizational structures along with text features are used by authors to share information. Point to new Anchor Chart with headings: chronology, comparisons, cause/effect, problem and solution.
- Go over the definition found in each form of structure.
- Read aloud text "Tribal Customs of the Shawnee, and Miami".
- Encourage student involvement by allowing times for students to turn and talk about text. Give a thinking stem or conversation prompt to encourage discussions.
- Use anchor chart and support students in selecting the correct organization structure; compare and contrast.
- Lead discussion as to why this organizational structure best fits the reading today.

Guided Practice
- Using Venn diagram chart, students will look at differences between tribal customs of Shawnee and Miami Indians.
- Students will write a response to "Why did the author choose to organize the information in this passage as compare and contrast?"
- Circulate room to listen to discussions and review responses.

Closure
- Bring students back together to share ideas and clear up any misunderstandings. Add article to anchor chart under compare and contrast.

Independent Practice
- Complete written statements at home if not completed in class. Completed statements due tomorrow.

Required Materials & Equipment
- Article, "Tribal Customs of Shawnee and Miami"
- Selection of articles that include a variety of text features, and organizational structures.
- Anchor chart & Venn Diagram charts

Assessment and Follow-Up
- Student sharing and observation of discussions
- Written responses: Why did the author choose to organize the information in this passage as compare and contrast?
- Exit Ticket – Name one of the examples of organizational structures you identified today and explain why it was an example of that structure.

It's not about the test

In their follow up meeting after completing their lesson Amanda and Kay discussed their reflections and shared what they felt worked well and what they might change in the future. They noticed a number of positives. They were both happy with the use of anchor charts. Their students enjoyed the group work and sharing their findings in class. Both teachers were pleased to see their students refer to the anchor charts throughout the unit. To accommodate the wide range of reading levels in both of their classes Amanda and Kay decided to use leveled text for independent practice. This strategy was a huge success and one that they will use again next year.

The lesson also had a few hiccups, and Amanda and Kay generated ideas to overcome these in the future. Amanda noted that her students' lack of knowledge about a topic interfered with their ability to focus on the organization of the text. Next year she wants to choose texts from the curriculum on topics they have already covered. This will allow her to reinforce the science and social studies content and allow students to focus on organization and structure rather than struggling with new information and vocabulary. Amanda and Kay also discovered that introducing more than one structure at a time took longer than focusing on one specific structure and then moving on to the next structure. Next year they will include additional examples of one type of organization structure across content before introducing other structures. As they walked around during the lesson, neither was satisfied with the enrichment activities. These students seemed disengaged, so Amanda and Kay agreed to consult with the fifth grade reading teachers to get ideas for an enrichment activity for next year.

It's not about the test

Mathematics

Read Ira's lesson plan.

Lesson Plan: 8th Grade Mathematics

Learning Targets
Prior Knowledge: Students converted rational numbers into fraction representations in a previous lesson.
Objective: 8.NS.A.1–Know that numbers that are not rational are called irrational. Understand informally that every number has a decimal expansion; for rational numbers show that the decimal expansion repeats eventually, and convert a decimal expansion which repeats eventually into a rational number.

Introduction
As students enter the class, ask them to write down on a sticky note anything that they know about rational or irrational numbers. Put the sticky notes on the correct chart on the board: Rational Numbers or Irrational Numbers. Go through the post-it as a class and move any that the group decides need to be moved. Leave this visual during up during the lesson and to refer back to at the end of the lesson.

Direct Instruction/Mini Lesson
• Show a number line and explain that between any two integers on the number line, there are an infinite number of rational and irrational numbers. Ask students to think of examples of rational and irrational numbers that fall between 3 and 4 and put them on the number line. Have these numbers ready to add to the number line in addition to what they come up with: π, 3 ½, 3.66666…, and √15. (Pi is important to include since students may think of 3.14 which is a shortened version of pi.)
• Review the definition of a rational number and introduce the definition of an irrational number.
    ○ Rational number—A number that can be expressed as an integer or a quotient of integers, excluding zero as a dnenominator.
    ○ Irrational number—A real number that cannot be expressed as a rational number.
• Look at examples of rational and irrational numbers. Have rational and irrational numbers printed on cards. In small groups, have students sort the cards into two piles, rational and irrational. For groups that finish that quickly, have them also sort the rational numbers into repeating and non-repeating decimals. Have students generate more examples for each category.

Guided Practice
Have students classify numbers as rational or irrational on a list provided. Then, students will place the numbers in the appropriate location on a number line. The following always/sometimes/never questions will be included. Students must answer always, sometimes, or never and give a reason.
○Rational numbers are always terminating or repeating decimals. *Always, must be represented as a ratio of two integers which will be a terminating or repeating decimal*
○Decimals go on forever without terminating or repeating. *Sometimes, pi does, ½ does not*
○Irrational numbers can be represented as a quotient of integers. *Never, it should say rational numbers.*

Closure
As a whole group, refer back to the original sticky note chart. Are there any changes that need to be made? Can we add any new sticky notes? Then, individually, complete the following exit ticket: *Use your own words to define rational and irrational numbers. Use examples to support your definition.*

Independent Practice
• Complete 10 of the corresponding problems in the textbook for homework.

Required Materials & Equipment
• T-Chart labeled "Rational Numbers" and "Irrational Numbers"
• Sticky Notes, list of rational and irrational numbers to classify
• Corresponding file for interactive whiteboard with vocabulary, number lines, and examples.

Assessment and Follow-Up
• Observation during discussions, group work, and guided practice
• Exit ticket and homework
• Summative assessment at the end of the unit

It's not about the test

After his rational and irrational number lesson, Ira is pleased with the overall results. All of his students could correctly define the two terms on their exit tickets. However, some of the students only provided examples that he had given to them during the lesson. Ira makes a note to monitor these students over the next few days to determine if they can to come up with other examples of rational and irrational numbers. He decided he would ask students to come up with an original example for the exit tickets next year. Using the sticky notes for the opening of the lesson and its closure worked well as it was easy to move and change responses that were not correct into the correct column. He did note a few places where students seemed to act bored or started talking. He made a note to add a transition, such as a quick interactive formative assessment.

Now you try:

Choose either Amanda or Ira's lesson plan. Determine the effectiveness of the lesson for addressing the targeted skill. What are your recommendations for changes or improvements?

Make a list of ten things you will watch for while teaching?

After your next lesson, jot down your thoughts about these ten things.

Choose one of your previously taught lesson plans. Create a list of things that went well that you want to remember to do again. Create a second list of weaknesses with action steps you think will strengthen your lesson plan or delivery.

Watch a colleague teach and ask him/her to watch you. Go through the list of ten things to watch for and reflect together.

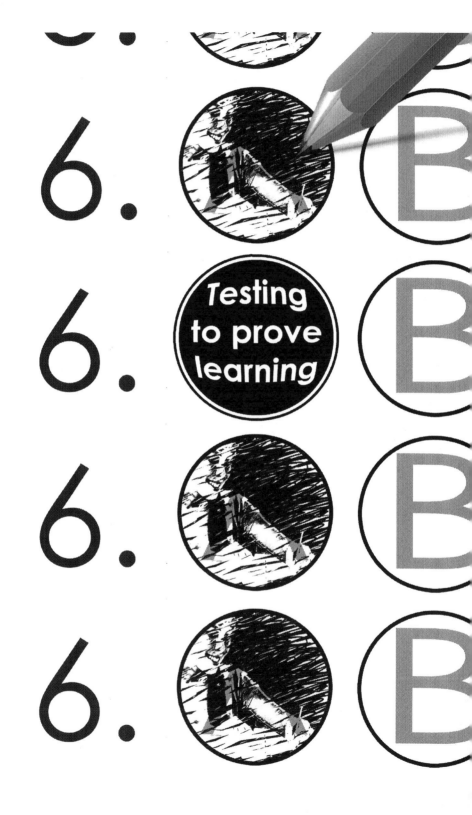

It's not about the test

Post testing, as its name implies, is intended to measure student learning after the instruction is completed. It provides students, teachers, administrators, and maybe even politicians and pundits with proof that learning occurred. The lesson's effectiveness (and some will say teacher's value) will be reflected in the student gains from the pretest to the posttest. A teacher can also use posttest results to identify students who still need intervention. Just as with pretest design, a well-designed post test can be a very useful tool to help you improve your practice.

Designing a good post test requires you consider "test intelligence (TQ)" and try to avoid creating items that require this type of intelligence. Instead of IQ, TQ includes the strategies and inside knowledge on how to take a test. Students learn to play the game, so their scores end up being a reflection on BOTH what they know and their TQ. Entire businesses make millions of dollars a year teaching kids to take tests, and the data on how these courses impact scores shows the importance of developing TQ. Tests that require high TQ do not yield an accurate measure of what the student has learned, so teachers need to consider how they can write items that are clearly understood by all students. When students miss questions because they do not understand what you are asking, you end up with bad data, which can lead teachers to very poor decision-making. Some students miss questions because they are nervous. The more teachers can create the final assessment to mirror the kinds of questions and formative assessment items they have used throughout the unit, the less likely a student is to be nervous or to misunderstand the question. Tests are a fact of life and are here to stay. They are now being used to judge school, classroom, and individual (student, teacher and principal) performance to inform increasingly high stakes decisions. So if test performance is made up of knowledge and TQ, teachers need to carefully consider how they design their assessments and work diligently to provide aligned and clear items.

Amanda and Kay know that some of the questions from the pretest were easy and, in fact, most of their students knew the answers. So they are considering dropping these questions from their posttest and replacing them with new test items covering what they have just taught in the lesson. Sounds like a plan, right?

Not really! By altering their posttest, they are making it more difficult to determine what their students learned and, inadvertently, missing an opportunity to let their students feel good about their learning.

Posttests should reflect EXACTLY the same material and the same level of difficulty, including the easy items, as your pretests. Refer back to your pretest plan and make sure you have the same distribution of questions that assess prerequisite skills, grade level skills and stretch questions. By using the same metric for your pretests and your posttests, you will be able to show student growth (and teacher value added). Additionally, and this is critical, your students get the positive feedback that is so valuable in the learning process. Your students will be able to what they learned and, in a very tangible way, the results of their efforts. Teachers can go through the items when they return the assessments and show students how they did on each type of question. Ideally, the teacher could give students three scores: the percentage of prerequisite questions they answered correctly, the percentage of grade level material they answered correctly and the percentage of the stretch questions they answered correctly. For the student's grade, teachers should only count the grade level percentage. This will help make grades a more accurate reflection of a student's level of mastery.

This practice will help students better understand what they know and what they still need to work on. For example, Ken Tankerous has his students create graphs of their individual progress; a kind-of before and after picture. His students love comparing their pretest scores to their posttest scores and discussing why and how they learned the material. Students gain confidence and motivation when they are able to reflect on how they learn and can see the impact their efforts have on their assessments. They can also discuss their learning process to reflect on what they did that led to learning. For example, a student might say, "When I listen to what Mrs. Dillon says and do the work, I can learn a lot. Just look at all the things I didn't know before, but that I know now! And, even though I did not get a score of 3 (proficient level) on the posttest I improved from a 1 to a 2. Amanda and Kay decide will maintain the same level of difficulty from their pretest to their posttest, but they will use a new passage and set of questions.

Ira decides to use reuse his pretest as his posttest and add a written response question to assess new skills. We do not recommend this practice, because it adds TQ. Teachers should review tests when they are returned to students. Students with a good memory for numbers will remember the right answers, especially on multiple choice questions. Ira will struggle to interpret the posttest data with confidence, because many students may have gotten the right answer because they remembered which answer was right, and not because they can reason through the problem. If Ira changes the numbers, but keeps the same format and same general items, he can overcome this issue and have a valid posttest.

Now you try:

To effectively demonstrate student growth, what elements are critical to include in the posttest?

What are the advantages and disadvantages to using a newly created post-test rather than using the initial pretest as the posttest?

Using your pretest as a guide, create a posttest you will use with your students.

It's not about the test

When teachers create sound pre and post assessments and use the data to inform instruction, powerful changes happen. Students become more engaged. Classrooms become more efficient. Student growth and achievement accelerates. However, some students continue to struggle, and teachers need to have backup plans to help those students reach mastery. Teachers need intervention plans they can employ for struggling students, and these plans can include different activities, leverage other adults, such as parent volunteers, or engage parents to help at home.

When posttest results indicate a student has not learned an important concept or standard, teachers need to design a back up plan that consists of interventions and additional opportunities for the student to learn. A back up plan is not the same as "re-teaching," which often consists simply of restating the original explanations louder and more slowly. A good back up plan looks at responses on pre- and posttests for insight into student thinking and accommodates differences in students' learning styles, learning modalities, or types of intelligence (Sternberg 1994).

An effective back up plan has three components (Guskey 1997).

1. It presents the standard differently. For example, if a language arts unit initially taught the use of metaphors in poetry with a deductive approach (presenting the general concept and then giving specific examples), your back up plan might use an inductive approach (presenting a variety of specific examples and building an understanding of the general concept from these examples). The best back up plans involve a change in format, organization, or method of presentation.

2. An effective back up plan engages students differently. If your science students initially learned about observations and inferences through a group activity, for example, a good back up plan might involve an individual activity, such as reviewing an informative website and then using the computer to write and illustrate a report. If students originally learned the events of the American Revolutionary War in social studies using their textbook and studying wall maps and charts, a back up plan might employ a group discussion of the events. To have an effective back up plan, students' engagement in learning must be qualitatively different from what took place during your initial instruction.

3. Finally, an effective back up plan should help students to overcome their learning difficulties and to experience success. Students should not fail twice.

The best ideas for effective corrective activities generally come from fellow teachers at grade level or department meetings. Your colleagues can offer new ways of presenting concepts, different examples, and alternative materials. A meeting devoted to examining posttest results and developing a backup plan is critical.

It's not about the test

This collaboration can only take place if you have gathered reliable data from your pre- and posttest.

A back up plan typically adds about 10-20% more time to a lesson (Block, Efthim, & Burns 1989). So if your lesson was a week in length, a back up plan might add another day. But you can usually get that time back since assistance offered early in an instructional sequence usually reduces the time needed for re-teaching in later lessons. The extra time you spend now will guarantee that your students have the learning prerequisites for subsequent lessons allowing you to cover just as much material as you would using more traditional methods (Guskey 2008).

After you have completed your back up plan, give students a second, parallel posttest to determine your intervention's effectiveness and offer students a second chance to demonstrate mastery and experience success. Again, distribution of item difficulty should be the same, but new questions, passages to read, or numbers in math problems is a much better idea than allowing a repeat of the exact same assessment. If students who struggled score well on the second chance, celebrate their success. They have learned just as much as the other students and, in many cases, had to work much harder to achieve success. Make sure you process with them what worked and encourage them to employ those strategies in the future, so they can score well on the first posttest.

Many teachers bristle at the idea of letting students continue to retake tests until they show mastery. If the point of a classroom is to get all students to march together in sync, then there should only be one chance. But that is not the purpose of education. The end goal is that all students learn the material, and any teacher will agree that students all learn at their own pace. Teachers' goal should be to help students reach mastery, period. If a student needs a practice test or extra time to get the concept to make sense, they should have it. Sound crazy? The driver's license examination offers a comparable example. Many individuals do not pass their driver's test on the first attempt. On the second or third try, however, they may reach the same high level of performance as others did on their first. The expectation is the same for everyone, but some drivers took longer to reach it. They eventually met the same high performance standards as those who passed on their initial attempt, so they receive the same privileges. Driver's licenses don't have a field to indicate whether or not the person passed the first time. The same should hold true for students who engage in corrective activities and eventually show that they, too, have learned well. Sadly what often happens is teachers reduce their expectations for the students who struggle and they never reach mastery.

As suggested in Step 5: Teach Teach Teach Teach, teachers should reflect upon their lessons. Once the posttest data comes in, another reflection is useful, so the lesson can be revised based on the test data as well as the information collected during teaching. Create an organization system where you can store your lessons and your reflections, so you can easily find them in future years. Each year you will build your lesson bank and back up plans until you have effective and engaging lessons for every unit. You and your colleagues will be able to continually add to your assessment item bank and back up plans each year. You would also build up historical data on each standard, so you would be able to more accurately predict student growth, which is helpful for teacher evaluations. In addition to making your classroom more efficient and responsive, you will enjoy accelerated student growth and achievement, better teacher evaluations, and enjoy more rewarding collaboration with your colleagues. As an added bonus, imagine what a nice gift these tried-and-true lessons and assessments could be for a novice teacher coming to your building next year. It would sure beat a box of donuts.

Each summer, as you get your classroom ready for students, teachers can spend time reviewing the previous year's data and considering how the scope and sequence in your curriculum map might need tweaked. The system you have learned in this book will ensure you have valid data, and if large numbers of students need back up plans, your team can reevaluate your lesson design, delivery, assessment questions, and support. This system also allows teachers to use data to select priority skills then collaborate with their colleagues to develop effective instruction and intervention. And teachers who move students from a score of 1 (well below proficient) to a score of 2 (approaching proficient) should get as much credit as teachers who move students from a score of 3 (proficient) to a score of 4 (advanced).

It's not about the test
See It in Action (Posttest Analysis)

Amanda and Kay are pleased to see that all their students showed growth, including students below grade level. In their posttest analysis, they identify the strengths and back up plans.

Domain/Topic/Standard RI.4.5 and RI.4.6				Date: 11/10/14	
Class Name	No understanding	Major Misconceptions or Errors	Minor Misconception or Errors	All Correct – Needs Enrichment	
Mrs. Dillon	0 students:	3 students: AL, JJ, GV	6 students	11 students	
Mr. Sera	0 students:	3 students: PA, DD, MM	5 students	12 students:	
Totals	0	6	11	23	

Pretest strengths, misconceptions, and student interests

Strengths:
- 100% of students demonstrated some understanding of organizing structures within text.
- 80% of students improved performance from pre to posttest
- 40% were able to use glossary to answer questions
- 23 (57%) were able to answer all questions correctly
- 3 (7%) students reading at below grade level improved ability to recognize structure to 3 out of 4 when materials were practiced and at instructional reading level.

Misconceptions or concerns with relevant instructional strategies (back up plan):
- 3 (7%) students remain below grade level in reading. (Recommended to Intervention Assistance Team for review of plan. Currently participating in corrective reading groups 3x per week)
- 6 (15%) students continue to confuse organizing structures, especially sequence and cause and effect. (Participate in additional small group work with high yield strategies including graphic organizers and comparisons based on similarities and differences; combine students for both classes when possible, look at joint schedules for best times.
- 27% still have some confusion regarding structures and missed 1 out of 3 questions (continue practice with articles as part of opening activities once a week for next month and add to anchor chart examples)

Domain/Topic/Standard RI.4.5 and RI.4.6						Date: 12/6/14		
Class Name	No understanding		Major Misconceptions or Errors		Minor Misconception or Errors		All Correct – Needs Enrichment	
	Pre	Post	Pre	Post	Pre	Post	Pre	Post
1A	2	0	7	3	10	6	1	11
1B	1	0	11	3	7	5	1	12
Totals	3	0	18	6	17	11	2	23

It's not about the test
Mathematics Post Test Analysis

Ira knows he still has work to do but he is pleased with his posttest results. All students made positive growth and nearly half have a clear understanding of the skills taught. Several students still have minor misconceptions due to errors in division when converting the fractions to decimals. Ira will have these students continue to practice converting to decimals with division.

Domain/Topic/Standard 8.NS.A.1, 8.NS.A.2			Date: 11/5/14	
Class Name	No understanding	Major Misconceptions or Errors	Minor Misconception or Errors	All Correct – Needs Enrichment
1A	0 students	1 student	8 students	10 students
1B	0 students	2 students	9 students	10 students
Totals	0	3	17	20
Pretest strengths, misconceptions, and student interests				

Strengths:
- 50% of the students earned perfect scores
- All students have at least some understanding of the content
- All but one students' scores increased from the pretest to the posttest

Misconceptions or concerns with relevant instructional strategies (back up plan):
- The minor misconceptions are due to errors in division when converting the factions to decimals. Students will continue to practice converting to decimals with division. Using a calculator will be helpful for these students also.
- Seven students with major misconceptions are having trouble placing rational and irrational numbers on the number line and differentiating between which numbers should be integers or whole numbers. Students will go over the errors on the assessment and practice related problems in small groups using a variety of strategies and tools.
- Layla's score went down from the pretest to the posttest. She will receive individual instruction after school on the topic to address the concerns.

Domain/Topic/Standard 8.NS.A.1, 8.NS.A.2							Date: 11/5/14	
Class Name	No understanding		Major Misconceptions or Errors		Minor Misconception or Errors		All Correct – Needs Enrichment	
	Pre	Post	Pre	Post	Pre	Post	Pre	Post
1A	1	0	8	1	9	8	1	10
1B	2	0	10	2	8	9	1	10
Totals	3	0	18	3	17	17	2	20

It's not about the test

Now you try:

Examine a posttest you have recently given and reflect upon the data it generates. How can changes to the assessment yield more usable data to improve instruction and increase student learning?

Look at Guskey's three components of an effective back-up plan. List the back up plans you use with struggling students.

Look at the post test analyses, identify two or more remaining instructional needs and create a back up plan for each.

It's not about the test
Compliance versus Commitment

When historians get around to listing the most astonishing discovery about school effectiveness, here is one finding that won't make their list: The road to "Academic Emergency" and low student achievement was paved with good intentions and good plans. Sadly what might make our "historians" list of astonishing discoveries is that we knew all along that good intentions and good plans were only half the battle. We knew implementing those plans represented the other half yet we rarely paid enough attention to this activity.

Last month we were asked to do a Design/Data Team workshop for a school district. The new curriculum director described how teachers were feeling frustrated concerning test analysis and collaboration. As she described the district to us, many of the school names sounded familiar. We checked our list of old contracts and discovered that we had been to her district in 2010. Turnover can be an issue in districts but surely not everyone had left!

How does this happen? We use the same power point slides, the same activities and see the same teacher enthusiasm in all our workshops. But it's after we turn off the projector, take down the chart paper and fold up the chairs that the rest of the work occurs. Some districts and dioceses do that work and take off while others don't and drift back to old habits or never leave the ground.

Planning to do something has always been much more energizing and exciting than actually doing it. Type the word "planning" into Amazon.com and nearly 253,000 results will pop up. The word "implementing" produces only 9,000.

There are a number of reasons implementation doesn't happen, but often the biggest barrier to a commitment to our system is the compliance protocol districts create. Administrators generate forms and try to force every teacher into a standardized process. Nothing kills creativity faster than forms. The important part of this system is NOT the forms. The important part is that teachers work together, improve their assessments so they are aligned and can generate useful data, and that they use that data to improve their instruction. The role of the administration is to ensure teachers have the time they need to collaborate, share data and work together. Their role is not to micromanage the discussions or squelch creative solutions because the logistics might be a bit tricky. We encourage administrators to celebrate this process by giving teachers time to work together and then share their progress to the entire staff. When we give teachers some autonomy to create solutions and own them, a real commitment to reform begins. When data team meetings become the place where great solutions were once considered and then discarded is discounted, the meetings will become another compliance driven activity with little yield. Educators talk about individualized instruction, personalized education and mastery for all, but if schools do not allow teachers to have the power to make instructional changes to accommodate various learners, then this talk is just fantasy. To walk the talk, teachers need to have the ability to be nimble and address their honest bad news with creative and innovative interventions.

There is a role in all this for administration, and that is at the building level. When successful data teams are working, the data can roll up to a building level team. Building data teams are a key ingredient for successful implementation. The building data team is a school-based group of teachers who support and monitor your data team plan and the smaller instructional data teams (Higgins et al, 2010).

The building data team organizes and manages the data decision making process within the building. The building data team's focus is on the entire building; what is working and what is not, for the entire building as well as individual grades or content areas. The building data team makes sure the instructional data teams have what they need (data, training, time, resources) to create and execute the plan for their subjects/grades. They do not become the compliance police or the form makers. Rather, they support big change. If teacher level teams are seeing that a particular part of the curriculum is always their honest bad news, the building level data team might examine the curricular materials and the vertical progression of that part of the curriculum to determine where the problem starts. Then they might advocate for new materials or bring in professional development to help the teachers troubleshoot various approaches and methods. The building data team is both coach and cheerleader to your instructional data teams.

The instructional teams use data to create plans, implement plans, determine the success of their plans and make adjustments as needed based on results. Their plans and results are shared with the building data team for feedback and additional support if needed. Working together, these two teams can address student needs at the building level, grade/subject level and individual level to maximize achievement and growth for all students in their school.

In Amanda and Kay's school, the building leadership team meets in August to define their primary role of implementing the instructional data teams. They use an implementation checklist to help them define their work, and then they revisit this checklist throughout the year to make sure work is moving forward. The teacher data teams also use a checklist to ensure they are productive.

It's not about the test

Building Data Teams Implementation Checklist

Step	Current State: where we are	Desired State: where we want to be	Our Action Plan: how we will get where we want to be
PLAN			
Form Building Data Teams and schedule meetings	in progress	Schedule in place by Sept.	Make sure our team represents all stakeholders.
Place meeting times for all teams on school calendar for the year	in progress	Schedule in place by Sept.	
Assign Team Roles for Building Data Team	not started	by 1st Sept. meeting	Make sure teams know what their role is.
Establish and communicate team norms	in progress	by 1st Sept. meeting	Principal shared checklist.
Create list of assessments; summative, formative, screeners, and diagnostic.....	in progress	by Oct. meeting	Team of teachers will complete this task.
Create schedule to administer assessments, identify staff to administer assessments and record data	completed		On school calendar.
Create method of recording and sharing data for analysis	do not have	would like in place Nov. 1	Invite school psychologist to October meeting.
DO			
Analyze building data to determine Success Stories and Honest Bad News; grade, subject, sub-groups....	in progress; only use state assessment data now	analyze district and class assessments also	Assign teams to discuss data from the list of assessments developed above. Progress will be reported to the Building Data Team.
Choose target area(s) for building, develop building wide improvement plan (align with district improvement plan)	not in place		Grade levels currently reviewing data. Need to identify building trends.
Select building goal/goals and how goals will be assessed/monitored to determine progress	not started	by November meeting	Review building data and instructional team data.
Create schedules and resources to support implementation of strategies & plans building wide.	not started	by December	Would like schedule and resources assigned by 2nd semester.

It's not about the test

Building Data Teams Implementation Checklist page 2

Step	Current State: where we are	Desired State: where we want to be	Our Action Plan: how we will get where we want to be
DO (Continued)			
Identify and communicate researched based instructional strategies to support building goals for targeted content	in progress	create a database of instructional strategies	Small group of teachers attended an effective teacher workshop.
Create list of researched based interventions/programs to support RTI data needs; communicate to staff	not started		Get this from intervention specialists and school psychologist.
CHECK			
Monitor implementation of instructional strategies and interventions; fidelity checks	minimal, only principal is involved now	have building leadership team participate	Leadership team members can participate in walk-throughs, data from walk-throughs can be shared with all.
Review data supplied by Instructional Data Teams and provide feedback	minimal, only principal is involved now	have building leadership team participate	Also complete during building leadership team meeting.
Review data supplied by Intervention Assistance Teams and provide feedback	in progress; only use state assessment data now		Work with school psychologist.
Create system for keeping track of results at all levels	not started	have building leadership team participate	Discuss options with district communication director and create a plan.
Create an in school communication system to share results and recommendations	not started	have building leadership team participate	Discuss options with district communication director and create a plan.
Create a district/community communication system	not started	have building leadership team participate	Discuss options with district communication director and create a plan.

It's not about the test

Instructional/Grade Level Teams Implementation Checklist

Step	Current State: where we are	Desired State: where we want to be	Our Action Plan: how we will get where we want to be
PLAN			
Form Instructional Data Teams	completed in Sept.		Two fourth grade teachers and principal
Assign team roles and responsibilites	completed in Sept.		Rotate and share responsibilities.
Schedule meetings for year if not already on building calendar; recommended 2x month	in progress		One meeting already on calendar, need to add other dates
Establish and communicate team norms	completed in Sept.		First meeting will be devoted to this.
DO			
Review data from BDT, building trends, grade level results, and benchmark data	completed in Sept.		Use Iowa Assessments.
Analyze data to uncover Success Stories and Honest Bad News.	completed		
Select target standard/indicators to address during school year based on honest bad news	chose standards for 1st and 2nd semester		Review standards for second semester in December.
Develop yearly Curriculum Calendars include schedule and intentional plan for instructing target area	completed		Completed by Oct. 1
Develop and administer Common Formative (pre) Assessments	completed November 1		Develop: Nov. 1
Administer: Nov. 16
Score Assessment, analyze data for strengths and misconceptions	completed		Met on Nov. 18

It's not about the test

Instructional/Grade Level Teams Implementation Checklist page 2

Step	Current State: where we are	Desired State: where we want to be	Our Action Plan: how we will get where we want to be
DO (Continued)			
Create common lesson plan based on assessment results, identify instructional strategies to be included in lesson	created Nov. 19		Allow more time between pretest and lesson. Felt rushed.
Share observations following shared lesson plan; make recommendations for adjustments/modifications to lesson	met and shared on Dec. 10		Share results and create posttest at same time.
Develop and Administer Common Post-Assessments	developed test Dec. 10		Administered on Dec. 17.
Analyze Post Assessments; Meet to determine if goal was met; strengths and continued misconceptions	Dec. 19		Too much scheduled to complete before winter break.
Develop back up plan for students not meeting goal on content standards on post assessments	Dec. 19		Too much scheduled to complete before winter break.
Communicate meeting notes and results/actions to BDT	on going		Meet with principal to share pre-to-posttest analysis table.
CHECK			
Create system for keeping track of results i.e. charts/graphs Form- ative assessments and progress monitoring of	in progress		Use pre-to-posttest analysis table to share with teams and principal.
Monitor progress of student results of common formative and summative assessments on identified targeted skills	need to develop		Meet with school psychologist for charting ideas.
Monitor progress on tiered interventions; apply decision rules for change as needed, include referral of individuals to	need to develop		Invite intervention specialists to meeting.
Create an in school communication system to share results with BDT for feedback and recommendations	need to develop		Ask building leadership team for help.

It's not about the test

The data-based and collaborative system we have described in this book asks teachers to consider how they can transform their schools to a place where assessment's primary role is to inform and improve instruction and where teachers work in teams to share, collaborate, and improve their practice. This shift can restore some joy in teaching and can elevate the perception of the profession and ensure teachers are equipped to truly educate every child. It can make schools a place where it's not about the test…it's about the learning.

It's not about the test

References

"Assess2Know." Harcourt Houghton Mifflin, 2013.

Bessie, Adam. "The Myth of the Bad Teacher." Truthout, October 2010.

Block, J, Efthim, H. & Burns, A. Mastery Learning Schools, Longman, 1989.

Guskey, Thomas. Implementing Mastery Learning, Wadsworth Publishing, 1997.

Guskey, Thomas. "The Rest of the Story." Educational Leadership, January, 2008.

Hattie, John. Visible Learning: A Synthesis of over 800 Meta-Analyses relating to Achievement. Routledge, 2009.

Higgins, M., Young, L., Weiner, J. & Wlodarczyk, S. "Leading teams of leaders: What helps team member learning?" Phi Delta Kappan, April, 2010.

"Iowa Assessments." Houghton Mifflin Harcourt, 2012.

Johnson, Susan Moore. "Having it Both Ways: Building the Capacity of Individual Teachers and their Schools" Harvard Educational Review, Spring, 2012.

Museum, John F. Kennedy Presidential Library and. Remarks the the Dedication of the Aerospace Medical Health Center (November 1963).

Padgett, Ken. "The History of Thomas Edison's Research Laboratory." Agile Writer, 2012.

Pfeffer, J & Sutton R. Hard Facts. Harvard Business School Press, 2006.

Stiggins, Rick. "New Assessment Beliefs for a new School Year." Phi Delta Kappan, September, 2004.

Sternberg, R. "Allowing for Thinking Styles." Educational Leadership, Spring, 1994.

It's not about the test
Resources

Initial Data Reflection Sheet

Yearly Planning Guide

Monthly Planning Guide

Pretest Planning Guide

Pretest Analysis

Lesson Plan Template

Posttest Analysis

Pre- to Posttest Analysis

Implementation Checklists

It's not about the test

Initial Data Reflection Sheet

Name(s) _____ Subject: _____ Date: _____

Success Stories

Honest Bad News

Anything Else

It's not about the test

Yearly Planning Guide: _____

Week of...	Unit/Topic	Standards	Notes

It's not about the test

Monthly Planning Guide: _____

Week of...	Standards and Summary of Plan

It's not about the test

Pretest Planning Guide: _____

When creating a pretest it is important to pre-assess the prerequisite skills needed before students will be able to master the new material. What skills do you expect students to have from the previous content or grade(s)? What new skills do the students need to develop or master?

Standards to be Addressed	Date to Administer Pretest	Prerequisite skills needed to teach listed content	Test Questions Include		
			Short Answer	Extended Response	Multiple Choice

It's not about the test

Pretest Analysis: _____

Directions: Use one sheet for each CCSS Standard or topic. List students in the appropriate section of the chart.

Domain/Topic/Standard:			Date:	
Class Name	No Understanding	Major Misconception or Errors	Minor Misconception or Errors	All Correct- Needs Enrichment

Pretest strengths, misconceptions, and student interests

It's not about the test

Lesson Plan: _____

Learning Targets

Introduction

Direct Instruction/Mini Lesson

Guided Practice

Closure

Independent Practice

Required Materials & Equipment

Assessment and Follow-Up

It's not about the test

Posttest Analysis: _____

Directions: Use one sheet for each CCSS Standard or topic. List students in the appropriate section of the chart.

Domain/Topic/Standard:			Date:	
Class Name	No Understanding	Major Misconception or Errors	Minor Misconception or Errors	All Correct– Needs Enrichment

List misconceptions or errors and how you will address the misconceptions here.

It's not about the test

Pre- to Posttest Analysis: _____

Directions: Use one sheet for each CCSS Standard or topic. List student numbers in the appropriate section of the chart.

Domain/Topic/Standard:				Date:	
Class Name	No Understanding	Major Misconception or Errors	Minor Misconception or Errors	All Correct– Needs Enrichment	

It's not about the test

Building Data Teams Implementation Checklist

Step	Current State: where we are	Desired State: where we want to be	Our Action Plan: how we will get where we want to be
PLAN			
Form Building Data Teams and schedule meetings			
Place meeting times for all teams (BDT, IDT, IAT) on school calendar for the year			
Assign Team Roles for Building Data Team			
Establish and communicate team norms			
Create list of assessments; summative, formative, screeners, and diagnostic.....			
Create schedule to administer assessments, identify staff to administer assessments and record data			
Create method of recording and sharing data for analysis			
DO			
Analyze building data to determine Success Stories and Honest Bad News; grade, subject, sub-groups....			
Choose target area(s) for building, develop building wide improvement plan (align with district improvement plan)			
Select building goal/goals and how goals will be assessed/ monitored to determine progress			
Create schedules and resources to support implementation of strategies /plans building wide.			

Building Data Teams Implementation Checklist page 2

Step	Current State: where we are	Desired State: where we want to be	Our Action Plan: how we will get where we want to be
DO (Continued)			
Identify and communicate researched based instructional strategies to support building goals for targeted content			
Create list of researched based interventions/programs to support RTI data needs; communicate to staff			
CHECK			
Monitor implementation of instructional strategies and interventions; fidelity checks			
Review data supplied by Instructional Data Teams and provide feedback			
Review data supplied by Intervention Assistance Teams and provide feedback			
Create system for keeping track of results at all levels			
Create an in school communication system to share results and recommendations			
Create a district/community communication system			

It's not about the test

Instructional/Grade Level Teams Implementation Checklist

Step	Current State: where we are	Desired State: where we want to be	Our Action Plan: how we will get where we want to be
PLAN			
Form Instructional Data Teams			
Assign team roles and responsibilites			
Schedule meetings for year if not already on building calendar; recommended 2x month			
Establish and communicate team norms			
DO			
Review data from BDT, building trends, grade level results, and benchmark data			
Analyze data to uncover Success Stories and Honest Bad News.			
Select target standard/indicators to address during school year based on honest bad news			
Develop yearly Curriculum Calendars include schedule and intentional plan for instructing target area			
Develop and administer Common Formative (pre) Assessments			
Score Assessment, analyze data for strengths and misconceptions			

It's not about the test

Instructional/Grade Level Teams Implementation Checklist page 2

Step	Current State: where we are	Desired State: where we want to be	Our Action Plan: how we will get where we want to be
DO (Continued)			
Create common lesson plan based on assessment results, identify instructional strategies to be included in lesson			
Share observations following shared lesson plan; make recommendations for adjustments/modifications to lesson			
Develop and Administer Common Post-Assessments			
Analyze Post Assessments; Meet to determine if goal was met; strengths and continued misconceptions			
Develop back up plan for students not meeting goal on content standards on post assessments			
Communicate meeting notes and results/actions to BDT			
CHECK			
Create system for keeping track of results i.e. charts/graphs Formative assessments and progress monitoring of interventions			
Monitor progress of student results of common formative and summative assessments on identified targeted skills			
Monitor progress on tiered interventions; apply decision rules for change as needed, include referral of individuals to IAT			
Create an in school communication system to share results with BDT for feedback and recommendations			

Made in the USA
Middletown, DE
12 June 2017